ディクテーション活用

完全改訂版

# TOEIC® Test
# 単語 頻度順
# 徹底マスター

スコア
450→550→650をめざす
600+66の語と表現

井上 治
Paul Leeming
吉野 成美
Justin Harris

TSURUMI SHOTEN

### 自習用音声について

本書の自習用音声は以下よりダウンロードできます。予習，復習にご利用ください。

（2025年4月1日開始予定）

http://www.otowatsurumi.com/00608/

URLはブラウザのアドレスバーに直接入力して下さい。

# はじめに

　本書は、TOEIC® Test のスコアアップに役立つ単語演習帳として 2013 年に出版した『TOEIC® Test 単語 頻度順徹底マスター スコア 450▶550▶650 をめざす 600 語＋66 表現』の完全改訂版です。
　旧版では UNIT で 600 語（名詞 300、動詞 180、形容詞 100、副詞 20）と付録の形で 66 表現（熟語・構文・定型表現）を取り扱いましたが、本書では熟語・構文・定型表現の UNIT を新たに設けることで、UNIT で 600 の語と表現（名詞 300、動詞 140、形容詞 80、副詞 20、熟語・構文 40、定型表現 20）と付録の形で 66 の語と表現を取り扱います。
　本書は第 1 部として「スコア 450 ➡ 550 をめざす 300 の語と表現」と付録「TOEIC® Part 1 頻出の単語・熟語・定型表現 20」、第 2 部として「スコア 550 ➡ 650 をめざす 300 の語と表現」と付録「今後頻出が予想される名詞・定型表現 46」という二部構成になっています。
　本書の大きな特徴は、旧版から変わらない以下の 3 点です。

## ① 頻度順に並ぶ見出し語

　公式問題集を中心に分析を行い、単なる登場回数ではなく、問題を解く上でのキーセンテンスに含まれているかどうかを重視し、666 の語と表現を選びました。したがって、本書で学習後に受験すれば、これらの語と表現がスコアアップに役立つものであることを実感していただけると思います。
　UNIT ごとに同じ品詞（UNIT 14 は「定型表現」、UNIT 15 と 30 は「熟語・構文」）の 20 語（20 表現）ずつが取り扱われ、頻度順（同一頻度の場合はアルファベット順）に並んでいます。つまり、名詞では UNIT 1 の 1 語目 employee が頻出度 1 位、UNIT 3 の 1 語目 advertisement が頻出度 21 位ということになります。
　旧版からの改良点は、UNIT 以外でも、「TOEIC® Part 1 頻出 20」では名詞⇒動詞⇒表現、「頻出が予想される 46」では名詞⇒表現の順で頻度順に並べたところです。

## ② 1 つの見出し語に 1 つの訳語

　1 つの語に複数の訳語がついていると覚えにくい上に、日本語で解答する設問がない TOEIC® では訳語は 1 つ知っていれば十分なため、1 つの見出し語に訳語を 1 つだけつけています。また、1 つの語で複数の重要な意味をもつ語に関しては、その意味ごとに別の語とみなして収載しています。例えば、issue は名詞で「号」と「問題」、動詞で「発行する」として 3 回登場します。
　旧版からの改良点は、見やすく・覚えやすくするために、1. 動詞の「〜を」「〜に」等を省略した、2.「日本語化」しているものは不自然な訳語に変換せずに、feedback「意見」⇒「フィードバック」のようにカタカナ語を使ったところです。

## ③ 例文に繰り返し現れる見出し語

　すべての例文について 666 の語と表現をできる限り多く用いて作成していますので、繰り返して見る・覚えることを通して、それぞれの語と表現の定着度が高まるようになっています。
　旧版からの改良点は、1. TOEIC® でよく見る例文であることを最優先に、UNIT の見出し語として既

出かどうかにはこだわらず、666 の語と表現を例文に取り入れた、2. 例文を見やすくするために、見出し語と見出し表現のイタリック表記を止めたところです。

　それでは、次ページの「本書の使い方」をお読みいただき、早速学習を始めましょう。本書が「TOEIC® でのスコアアップに有益だ」とみなさんに感じていただけることを執筆者一同願ってやみません。

　最後になりましたが、音羽書房鶴見書店の佐藤信夫氏には、本書の出版にあたり謹んで感謝の意を表します。執筆の遅れを我慢強く待っていただき、本当にありがとうございました。

　また、本書の企画立案には、西谷恒志・マイケル・シャワティ編著『TOEIC® Test コア 300 Words』（音羽書房鶴見書店刊）が大きなヒントとなりました。改めてお二人に謝意を表します。

2024 年 11 月

執筆者代表　　井 上　治

# 本書の使い方

## ● UNIT の 1 ページ目

　ダウンロードした音声で 20 の見出し語・表現の発音練習をしたあと、枠内の語群から訳語を選んで書き込みます。自分で訳語を選んで書き込むことで、自分の中で定着している語、まだあいまいな語、これから覚えていく語を分けることができます。このページの表記のルールは次の通りです。

① UNIT 3 の advertisement [ad] のような表記は、角かっこ内のような略語として使われることも TOEIC® では多いことを、UNIT 5 の app [application] は略語として使われることの方が TOEIC® では多いことを示す。

② UNIT 3 の supplies のように、その訳語の場合には基本的に複数形で用いられる名詞については、複数形で表記する。

③ UNIT 6 の participate (in) のような表記は、その語・表現に丸かっこ内の前置詞が続くことが多いことを示す。

④ UNIT 1 の「顧客」と「顧客」、「商品」と「製品」のように、まったく同じ、あるいは類似の訳語がある場合は、小テストなどの際の混同を避けるため、訳語を区別する説明を角かっこで加える。

⑤ 角かっこは、UNIT 16「空き［仕事の］」のように、訳語の意味を補完する際にも用いる。

⑥ UNIT 1 の「契約（書）」のような丸かっこは、「契約」と「契約書」が場合に応じて使い分けられることを示す。

## ● UNIT の 2 ページ目と 3 ページ目

　20 の例文の音声を聴いて空所を埋めて、日本語訳の中でその語・表現の訳語に該当する部分を○で囲みます。この演習によって、見出し語・表現のつづりと訳語の定着度を確認できます。なお、各ページ下にそのページの空所に入る 10 の語・表現が表示されていますので活用してください。

　ただし、空所には見出し語・表現がそのまま入る場合と、名詞ならば複数形、動詞ならば三単現の s をつけたり、過去形や ing 形のように語形を変化させる場合がありますので注意が必要です。

　また、UNIT の見出し語・表現について、その例文の日本語訳中の訳語に関しては、見出し語・表現の訳語を用いると文意が取りにくくなる一部の例文を除いて、○で囲みやすくするために 1 ページ目の訳語を使用しています。

　一方、日本語訳を参考に空所を埋めたあとに音声で答え合わせをするという方法も効果的です。その答え合わせのあとに、音声を追いかけて例文の発音練習をしたり、例文のディクテーションをすれば、さらに効果的な学習となります。

## ● UNIT の 4 ページ目

　20 の見出し語・表現をいったん覚えたら、練習問題にチャレンジしましょう。3 種類の設問（類義語となる見出し語・表現を答える、見出し語の派生語を答える、TOEIC® の Part 5 形式）を通して、自分の中の定着度を確認してください。なお、UNIT の学習効果を高めるために、Part 5 形式の設問の合計 20 個の選択肢はその UNIT の見出し語・表現をすべて使用していますので、訳語がわからない語・表現があればそこでチェックを入れておいて、あとで 1 ページ目に戻って確認ができます。

● UNIT 以外の 66 の語と表現

　TOEIC® Part 1 特有の語・表現を「TOEIC® Part 1 頻出の単語・熟語・定型表現 20」として、TOEIC® では名詞を多く知っていると有利なので、頻出傾向にある名詞を「今後頻出が予想される名詞・定型表現 46」として収載しました。スコアアップに直結する語・表現ばかりですので、ぜひ習得してください。

　なお、単語の発音記号はアメリカ式の一般的なものを採用していますが、録音の音声はアメリカ人男性とイギリス人女性によるものです。

# 目　次

**第 1 部：スコア 450 ➡ 550 をめざす 300 の語と表現**

| UNIT 1 | 名　詞 1 | 3 |
| UNIT 2 | 動　詞 1 | 7 |
| UNIT 3 | 名　詞 2 | 11 |
| UNIT 4 | 名　詞 3 | 15 |
| UNIT 5 | 名　詞 4 | 19 |
| UNIT 6 | 動　詞 2 | 23 |
| UNIT 7 | 名　詞 5 | 27 |
| UNIT 8 | 形容詞 1 | 31 |
| UNIT 9 | 名　詞 6 | 35 |
| UNIT 10 | 動　詞 3 | 39 |
| UNIT 11 | 名　詞 7 | 43 |
| UNIT 12 | 動　詞 4 | 47 |
| UNIT 13 | 名　詞 8 | 51 |
| UNIT 14 | 定型表現 | 55 |
| UNIT 15 | 熟語・構文 1 | 59 |

❏ TOEIC® Part 1 頻出の単語・熟語・定型表現 20 ......... 63

**第 2 部：スコア 550 ➡ 650 をめざす 300 の語と表現**

| UNIT 16 | 名　詞 9 | 67 |
| UNIT 17 | 動　詞 5 | 71 |
| UNIT 18 | 名　詞 10 | 75 |
| UNIT 19 | 形容詞 2 | 79 |
| UNIT 20 | 名　詞 11 | 83 |
| UNIT 21 | 動　詞 6 | 87 |
| UNIT 22 | 名　詞 12 | 91 |
| UNIT 23 | 形容詞 3 | 95 |
| UNIT 24 | 名　詞 13 | 99 |
| UNIT 25 | 動　詞 7 | 103 |
| UNIT 26 | 名　詞 14 | 107 |
| UNIT 27 | 形容詞 4 | 111 |
| UNIT 28 | 名　詞 15 | 115 |
| UNIT 29 | 副　詞 | 119 |
| UNIT 30 | 熟語・構文 2 | 123 |

❏ 今後頻出が予想される名詞・定型表現 46 ......... 127

INDEX ......... 133

# 第1部

## スコア 450 ➡ 550 をめざす 300 の語と表現

# UNIT 1
## 名詞 1

**1-A** それぞれの英単語の意味に最も当てはまる日本語を選びましょう。

1) **employee** [ɪmplɔ́ii:]

2) **product** [prá:dəkt]

3) **customer** [kʌ́stəmər]

4) **client** [kláɪənt]

5) **conference** [ká:nfərəns]

6) **item** [áɪtəm]

7) **department** [dɪpá:rtmənt]

8) **equipment** [ɪkwípmənt]

9) **location** [loʊkéɪʃən]

10) **form** [fɔ́:rm]

11) **budget** [bʌ́dʒət]

12) **position** [pəzíʃən]

13) **policy** [pá:ləsi]

14) **marketing** [má:rkətɪŋ]

15) **advertising** [ǽdvərtáɪzɪŋ]

16) **contract** [ká:ntrækt]

17) **survey** [sə́:rveɪ]

18) **appointment** [əpɔ́ɪntmənt]

19) **article** [á:rtɪkl]

20) **reservation** [rèzərvéɪʃən]

---

| | | | |
|---|---|---|---|
| 会議 | 機器 | 記事 | 契約（書） |
| 広告 | 顧客［サービス・アドバイスを受ける］ | 顧客［物を買う］ | |
| 市場戦略 | 従業員 | 商品［具体的なひとつの］ | 職位 |
| 製品［生産品］ | 調査（票） | 場所 | 部署 |
| 方針 | 用紙 | 予算 | |
| 予約［人と会う・サービスを受ける約束］ | | 予約［ホテル・飛行機など、場所や席の確保］ | |

## 1-B 音声を聴き、英文の空所にあてはまる単語を入れ、その単語に該当する日本語を○で囲みましょう。
(単語は必要に応じて変化させましょう。)

🎧 03

1. Where should I set up the computer (　　　　　)?
   どこにコンピュータ機器を設置いたしましょうか。

2. Our Kyoto store has the (　　　　　) in stock.
   当方の京都の店舗にその商品の在庫がございます。

3. All (　　　　　) must attend the company awards ceremony.
   従業員全員が社の表彰式に出席しなければならない。

4. Fill out and submit an application (　　　　　).
   申込用紙に記入して提出してください。

5. How can (　　　　　) receive special discounts?
   どうすれば顧客は特別な割引を受けられますか。

🎧 04

6. George has been preparing for the annual sales (　　　　　).
   ジョージは年次販売会議の準備をしている。

7. The company announced the release of a new (　　　　　).
   その会社は新製品の発売を発表した。

8. The Italian restaurant moved to a new (　　　　　).
   そのイタリアンレストランは新しい場所に移転した。

9. The salesperson contacted some (　　　　　) regarding a problem.
   その販売員はある問題に関して顧客と連絡を取った。

10. What (　　　　　) do the speakers most likely work in?
    話し手たちはどの部署でおそらく働いていますか。

| ☐ client | ☐ department | ☐ form | ☐ product |
|---|---|---|---|
| ☐ conference | ☐ employee | ☐ item | |
| ☐ customer | ☐ equipment | ☐ location | |

## 1-C

音声を聴き、英文の空所にあてはまる単語を入れ、その単語に該当する日本語を○で囲みましょう。
（単語は必要に応じて変化させましょう。）

1. All ( contracts ) must be signed and returned to us.
   すべての契約書にご署名のうえ当方にお戻しいただきます。

2. John has been appointed as director of ( marketing ).
   ジョンは市場戦略部長に任命された。

3. Linda resigned from her ( position ) as CEO last month.
   リンダは先月最高経営責任者の職位を辞任した。

4. What does the ( article ) indicate about the firm?
   記事はその会社についてどのようなことを示唆していますか。

5. Mary presented the results of the ( survey ) she conducted.
   メアリーは自分が行った調査の結果を発表した。

6. We need to review the ( budget ) for the project.
   われわれはプロジェクトの予算を見直す必要がある。

7. I made a hotel ( reservation ) for my business trip.
   私は出張のためにホテルの予約をした。

8. She canceled a dental ( appointment ) due to urgent business.
   彼女は急用ができたために歯医者の予約をキャンセルした。

9. We will focus on television ( advertising ).
   当社はテレビでの広告に重点をおいて参ります。

10. The president explained a change to the hiring ( policy ).
    社長は雇用方針の変更を説明した。

---

☐ advertising ☐ budget ☐ policy ☐ survey
☐ appointment ☐ contract ☐ position
☐ article ☐ marketing ☐ reservation

UNIT 1／名詞1　5

## 1-D

● それぞれの語の類義語を、このUNITの見出し語から選びましょう。

1) agreement _____
2) customer _____
3) division _____
4) post _____
5) worker _____

● それぞれの語の動詞形を書きましょう。

1) equipment _____
2) location _____
3) product _____
4) reservation _____
5) survey _____

## 1-E

空所に入る最も適切な語を選びましょう。ただし、それぞれの語の意味はこのUNITで取り扱ったものとします。

1. Nancy is going to present at a trade ------ tomorrow.

    (A) conference    (B) contract    (C) product    (D) survey

2. I'd like to return an ------ because it is damaged.

    (A) appointment    (B) employee    (C) equipment    (D) item

3. Please pick up a copy of the ------ at the reception desk.

    (A) customer    (B) department    (C) form    (D) marketing

4. The ------ for this fiscal year has not yet been approved.

    (A) budget    (B) client    (C) location    (D) reservation

5. They discussed the cost of ------ at the meeting.

    (A) advertising    (B) article    (C) policy    (D) position

# UNIT 2
## 動詞 1

**2-A** それぞれの英単語の意味に最も当てはまる日本語を選びましょう。

1) **offer** [ɔ́(ː)fər] _____

2) **provide** [prəváɪd] _____

3) **include** [ɪnklúːd] _____

4) **hire** [háɪər] _____

5) **attend** [əténd] _____

6) **purchase** [pə́ːrtʃəs] _____

7) **complete** [kəmplíːt] _____

8) **update** [ʌpdéɪt] _____

9) **submit** [səbmít] _____

10) **require** [rɪkwáɪər] _____

11) **suggest** [səgdʒést] _____

12) **conduct** [kəndʌ́kt] _____

13) **order** [ɔ́ːrdər] _____

14) **add** [ǽd] _____

15) **review** [rɪvjúː] _____

16) **recommend** [rèkəménd] _____

17) **indicate** [índəkèɪt] _____

18) **confirm** [kənfə́ːrm] _____

19) **reduce** [rɪd(j)úːs] _____

20) **expect** [ɪkspékt] _____

---

| 行う | 確認する | 完了させる | 加える |
| 更新する | 購入する | 示す | 出席する |
| 勧める | 注文する | 提案する | 提供する［準備して与える］ |
| 提供する［積極的に差し出す］ | 提出する | 必要とする | 含む |
| 減らす | 見直す | 雇う | 予想する |

## 2-B
音声を聴き、英文の空所にあてはまる単語を入れ、その単語に該当する日本語を○で囲みましょう。
(単語は必要に応じて変化させましょう。)

🎧09

1. The fitness center ( purchased ) the latest exercise equipment.
   そのフィットネスセンターは最新の運動機器を購入した。

2. Anne ( updated ) the client mailing list the other day.
   アンは先日顧客メーリングリストを更新した。

3. We are pleased to ( offer ) you the position of human resources manager.
   当社は貴殿に人事課長の職位を謹んで提供いたします。

4. Reservations are ( required ) for dinner at our restaurant.
   当レストランではディナーには予約が必要です。

5. Our factory has to ( hire ) some temporary workers.
   われわれの工場は数名の臨時の従業員を雇わなければならない。

🎧10

6. The budget proposal must be ( submitted ) this afternoon.
   予算案は今日の午後に提出しなければならない。

7. What terms are ( included ) in the contract?
   その契約にはどのような条件が含まれていますか。

8. Jack is planning to ( attend ) a marketing conference.
   ジャックはマーケティング会議に出席するつもりです。

9. We ( provide ) information about our products on our website.
   当社ウェブサイトで当社製品についての情報を提供しています。

10. New employees must ( complete ) their on-the-job training.
    新入社員は実地訓練を完了しなければならない。

| ☐ attend | ☐ include | ☐ purchase | ☐ update |
| ☐ complete | ☐ offer | ☐ require | |
| ☐ hire | ☐ provide | ☐ submit | |

## 2-C 音声を聴き、英文の空所にあてはまる単語を入れ、その単語に該当する日本語を○で囲みましょう。
（単語は必要に応じて変化させましょう。）

1. The president ( ) extra information to the brochure.
社長はパンフレットに追加の情報を加えた。

2. What does the speaker ( ) the listeners do?
話し手は聞き手が何をすることを勧めていますか。

3. I'm calling to ( ) your appointment for tomorrow.
明日のご予約の確認をさせていただくためにお電話を差し上げています。

4. The supermarket ( ) a customer satisfaction survey.
そのスーパーは顧客満足度調査を行った。

5. Our company needs to ( ) its operating costs.
わが社は業務コストを削減する必要がある。

6. James ( ) starting a new advertising campaign.
ジェイムズは新しい広告キャンペーンを始めることを提案した。

7. We ( ) a large crowd at today's championship parade.
われわれは本日の優勝パレードで多くの人出を予想している。

8. The company ( ) some of its vacation policies.
その会社は休暇に関する方針の一部を見直した。

9. The item you ( ) is currently out of stock.
ご注文いただいた商品は現在在庫がございません。

10. What does the article ( ) about the new CEO?
記事はその新しいCEOについてどのようなことを示していますか。

| ☐ add | ☐ expect | ☐ recommend | ☐ suggest |
|---|---|---|---|
| ☐ conduct | ☐ indicate | ☐ reduce | |
| ☐ confirm | ☐ order | ☐ review | |

## 2-D

- それぞれの語の類義語を、この UNIT の見出し語から選びましょう。

1) buy　　　_____
2) cut　　　_____
3) do　　　_____
4) employ　_____
5) need　　_____

- それぞれの語の名詞形を書きましょう。

1) attend　　_____
2) complete　_____
3) recommend _____
4) submit　　_____
5) suggest　　_____

## 2-E

空所に入る最も適切な語を選びましょう。ただし、それぞれの語の意味はこの UNIT で取り扱ったものとします。

1. Does the price of the refrigerator ------ delivery and installation?

    (A) add　　(B) include　　(C) review　　(D) update

2. I'm writing to ------ you with a schedule of presentations.

    (A) complete　　(B) provide　　(C) require　　(D) suggest

3. Please sign below to ------ your acceptance of the job offer.

    (A) expect　　(B) indicate　　(C) order　　(D) recommend

4. The store plans to ------ free original goods to the first 100 customers.

    (A) conduct　　(B) hire　　(C) offer　　(D) submit

5. He forgot to ------ the date and time of the final interview.

    (A) attend　　(B) confirm　　(C) purchase　　(D) reduce

# UNIT 3
## 名詞 2

**3-A** それぞれの英単語の意味に最も当てはまる日本語を選びましょう。

1) advertisement [ad] [ædvərtáɪzmənt]
2) award [əwɔ́ːrd]
3) fee [fíː]
4) material [mətíəriəl]
5) workshop [wə́ːrkʃɑ̀p]
6) payment [péɪmənt]
7) review [rɪvjúː]
8) construction [kənstrʌ́kʃən]
9) facility [fəsíləti]
10) purchase [pə́ːrtʃəs]
11) supplies [səpláɪz]
12) document [dɑ́ːkjəmənt]
13) firm [fə́ːrm]
14) shipping [ʃípɪŋ]
15) colleague [kɑ́ːliːɡ]
16) community [kəmjúːnəti]
17) production [prədʌ́kʃən]
18) deadline [dédlaɪn]
19) location [loʊkéɪʃən]
20) vehicle [víːəkl]

| | | | |
|---|---|---|---|
| 会社 | 建設 | 広告 | 講習会 |
| 購入 (品) | 材料 | 施設 | 支払い |
| 締め切り | 車両 | 賞 | 生産 (量) |
| 地域社会 | 店舗 | 同僚 | 配送 |
| 批評 | 文書 | 用品 | 料金 |

## 3-B

音声を聴き、英文の空所にあてはまる単語を入れ、その単語に該当する日本語を○で囲みましょう。
（単語は必要に応じて変化させましょう。）

🎧 15

1. Our restaurant charges a 10 percent service (　　　　　).
   当レストランは 10 パーセントのサービス料を頂戴しております。

2. Matt has created some attractive television (　　　　　).
   マットは人の目を引き付けるテレビ広告を作り出してきた。

3. (　　　　　) will be due on delivery.
   お支払いは配達の際にお願いいたします。

4. You can use the coupon for online (　　　　　).
   そのクーポンはオンラインでの購入に使うことができます。

5. (　　　　　) of the bridge will be completed soon.
   その橋の建設はまもなく完了します。

🎧 16

6. Jane led a marketing (　　　　　) for new employees.
   ジェインは新入社員向けのマーケティング講習会を取り仕切った。

7. They gave us a tour of the (　　　　　).
   彼らはわれわれに施設をひととおり案内してくれた。

8. The actor is expected to win the (　　　　　).
   その俳優はその賞を獲得すると思われている。

9. Some of the raw (　　　　　) have not yet arrived.
   原材料の一部がまだ届いていません。

10. Most (　　　　　) of the play have been positive.
    その劇のほとんどの批評は好意的だ。

| ☐ advertisement | ☐ facility | ☐ payment | ☐ workshop |
| ☐ award | ☐ fee | ☐ purchase | |
| ☐ construction | ☐ material | ☐ review | |

## 3-C 音声を聴き、英文の空所にあてはまる単語を入れ、その単語に該当する日本語を○で囲みましょう。
（単語は必要に応じて変化させましょう。）

🎧17

1. Mike assisted his ( colleagues ) with their presentation.
   マイクは同僚たちのプレゼンを手伝った。

2. Should I order office ( supplies ) now or later?
   事務用品は今注文しましょうか、それとも後でしましょうか。

3. Nancy purchased a small, fuel-efficient ( vehicle ).
   ナンシーはコンパクトで燃料効率の良い車両を購入した。

4. The factory needs to increase ( production ) by 20 percent.
   その工場は生産を20パーセント増やす必要がある。

5. Sally corrected a mistake in the ( document ) David sent.
   サリーはデイビッドが送ってきた文書のまちがいを訂正した。

🎧18

6. Our electronics store offers free same-day ( shipping ).
   当家電店は当日配送を無料で提供しております。

7. The department had to meet a tight ( deadline ).
   その部署はタイトな締め切りに間に合わせなければならなかった。

8. Our company has supported various projects in the ( community ).
   当社は地域社会でのさまざまなプロジェクトを支援して参りました。

9. This is a great opportunity for our publishing ( firm ).
   今回はわたくしどもの出版社にとってすばらしい機会です。

10. Today is the grand opening of our new ( location ).
    今日は私たちの新店舗のグランドオープンです。

---

☐ colleague ☐ document ☐ production ☐ vehicle
☐ community ☐ firm ☐ shipping ☐ supplies
☐ deadline ☐ location

UNIT 3／名詞2

## 3-D

- それぞれの語の類義語を、このUNITの見出し語から選びましょう。

1) company _____
2) rate _____
3) paper _____
4) prize _____
5) seminar _____

- それぞれの語の動詞形を書きましょう。

1) advertisement _____
2) construction _____
3) payment _____
4) purchase _____
5) shipping _____

## 3-E

空所に入る最も適切な語を選びましょう。ただし、それぞれの語の意味はこのUNITで取り扱ったものとします。

**1.** We don't carry that item at our Umeda ------.

(A) award　　(B) location　　(C) production　　(D) purchase

**2.** Our boss requested an extension of the project ------.

(A) deadline　　(B) material　　(C) shipping　　(D) vehicle

**3.** Cathy picked up her ------ at the station because it was raining.

(A) colleague　　(B) firm　　(C) review　　(D) workshop

**4.** Ray placed an order for party ------ on the internet.

(A) community　　(B) construction　　(C) payment　　(D) supplies

**5.** Employees have free access to the nearby fitness ------.

(A) advertisement　　(B) document　　(C) facility　　(D) fee

# UNIT 4
## 名詞 3

**4-A** それぞれの英単語の意味に最も当てはまる日本語を選びましょう。

🎧 19

1) **maintenance** [méɪntənəns] _____

2) **security** [sɪkjúərəti] _____

3) **session** [séʃən] _____

4) **supervisor** [súːpərvàɪzər] _____

5) **clothing** [klóʊðɪŋ] _____

6) **interview** [íntərvjùː] _____

7) **notice** [nóʊtəs] _____

8) **opportunity** [àːpərt(j)úːnəti] _____

9) **option** [áːpʃən] _____

10) **feedback** [fíːdbæk] _____

🎧 20

11) **detail** [díːteɪl] _____

12) **package** [pǽkɪdʒ] _____

13) **property** [práːpərti] _____

14) **identification [ID]** [aɪdèntəfɪkéɪʃən] _____

15) **industry** [índəstri] _____

16) **shipment** [ʃípmənt] _____

17) **accounting** [əkáʊntɪŋ] _____

18) **agency** [éɪdʒənsi] _____

19) **participant** [pɑːrtísəpənt] _____

20) **application** [æ̀plɪkéɪʃən] _____

---

| 衣類 | 会合 | 機会 | 業界 |
| 警備 | 経理 | 小包 | 参加者 |
| 詳細 | 上司 | 選択肢 | 代理店 |
| 通知 | 発送（品） | フィードバック | 不動産 |
| 保守整備 | 身分証明（書） | 面接 | 申し込み（用紙） |

## 4-B
音声を聴き、英文の空所にあてはまる単語を入れ、その単語に該当する日本語を○で囲みましょう。
（単語は必要に応じて変化させましょう。）

🎧 21

1. Emily signed up for the (　　　　　　) in advance.
   エミリーはその会合に前もって参加登録をした。

2. Tom posted the (　　　　　　) on the bulletin board.
   トムは掲示板にその通知を掲示した。

3. Our restaurant offers a variety of food delivery (　　　　　　).
   当レストランはバラエティに富んだデリバリー用の料理の選択肢を提供しております。

4. I'll let our (　　　　　　) know about the schedule change.
   私が上司にスケジュールの変更について知らせます。

5. She conducted (　　　　　　) with some job candidates.
   彼女は仕事の応募者数名と面接を行なった。

🎧 22

6. We're collecting customer (　　　　　　) about our new product.
   当社の新製品に関する顧客からのフィードバックを募っているところです。

7. The community center is closed for routine (　　　　　　).
   コミュニティセンターは定期の保守整備のために閉鎖されている。

8. Our company provides (　　　　　　) for professional development.
   わが社は職能開発の機会を提供している。

9. The company manufactures (　　　　　　) and equipment for mountain climbing.
   その会社は登山用の衣類と用具を製造している。

10. We need to improve (　　　　　　) within the museum.
    われわれは美術館内の警備を改善する必要がある。

---

| ☐ clothing | ☐ maintenance | ☐ option | ☐ supervisor |
| ☐ feedback | ☐ notice | ☐ security | |
| ☐ interview | ☐ opportunity | ☐ session | |

## 4-C
音声を聴き、英文の空所にあてはまる単語を入れ、その単語に該当する日本語を○で囲みましょう。
（単語は必要に応じて変化させましょう。）

1. He picked up a ( package ) at the post office.
   彼は郵便局で小包を取ってきた。

2. Kate presented her photo ( identification ) at reception.
   ケイトは受付で顔写真付きの身分証明を提示した。

3. We expect more conference ( participants ) this year.
   われわれは今年はより多くの会議への参加者を期待している。

4. I'd like to look at some commercial ( properties ).
   商業用不動産をいくつか見てみたいのですが。

5. Laura learned the basics of ( accounting ) during the workshop.
   ローラはその講習会で経理の基本を学んだ。

6. ( Applications ) received after the deadline will not be accepted.
   締め切り後に受け取った申し込みは受理されません。

7. I apologize for not giving you sufficient ( details ).
   みなさまに十分な詳細をお伝えしなかったことを謝罪いたします。

8. Jim has been working at an advertising ( agency ).
   ジムはずっと広告代理店に勤めている。

9. She is concerned about the delayed ( shipment ).
   彼女は発送が遅れていることを心配している。

10. In what ( industry ) are the speakers most likely employed?
    話し手たちはおそらくどの業界で雇用されていますか。

☐ accounting    ☐ detail          ☐ package      ☐ shipment
☐ agency        ☐ identification  ☐ participant  
☐ application   ☐ industry        ☐ property

## 4-D

● それぞれの語の類義語を、このUNITの見出し語から選びましょう。

1) apparel _____
2) chance _____
3) choice _____
4) meeting _____
5) particular _____

● それぞれの語の動詞形を書きましょう。

1) application _____
2) identification _____
3) maintenance _____
4) participant _____
5) supervisor _____

## 4-E

空所に入る最も適切な語を選びましょう。ただし、それぞれの語の意味はこのUNITで取り扱ったものとします。

1. The schedule for the conference may be subject to change without ------.

   (A) accounting     (B) interview     (C) notice     (D) session

2. The mayor built a new library based on community ------.

   (A) feedback     (B) identification     (C) option     (D) participant

3. The ------ is conveniently located in the center of the city.

   (A) detail     (B) maintenance     (C) opportunity     (D) property

4. The woman is a highly respected designer in the fashion ------.

   (A) application     (B) industry     (C) package     (D) supervisor

5. I purchased bullet train tickets at a local travel ------.

   (A) agency     (B) clothing     (C) security     (D) shipment

# UNIT 5
## 名詞 4

**5-A** それぞれの英単語の意味に最も当てはまる日本語を選びましょう。

1) **candidate** [kǽndədèɪt]
2) **proposal** [prəpóʊzl]
3) **renovation** [rènəvéɪʃən]
4) **invoice** [ínvɔɪs]
5) **merchandise** [mə́ːrtʃəndàɪz]
6) **representative** [rèprɪzéntətɪv]
7) **resident** [rézədənt]
8) **expense** [ɪkspéns]
9) **feature** [fíːtʃər]
10) **management** [mǽnɪdʒmənt]

11) **packaging** [pǽkɪdʒɪŋ]
12) **amount** [əmáʊnt]
13) **app [application]** [ǽp]
14) **device** [dɪváɪs]
15) **estimate** [éstəmət]
16) **refund** [ríːfʌnd]
17) **transportation** [trænspərtéɪʃən]
18) **convention** [kənvénʃən]
19) **development** [dɪvéləpmənt]
20) **material** [mətíəriəl]

| | | | |
|---|---|---|---|
| アプリ | 応募者 | 送り状 | 開発 |
| 経営 | 経費 | 交通機関 | 住民 |
| 商品 | 資料 | 装置 | 大会 |
| 担当者 | 提案 | 特徴 | 返金 |
| 包装（材） | 見積もり | リフォーム | 量 |

## 5-B
音声を聴き、英文の空所にあてはまる単語を入れ、その単語に該当する日本語を○で囲みましょう。
（単語は必要に応じて変化させましょう。）

🎧 27

1. Your purchase information is on the (　　　　　).
   お客様の購入品の情報は送り状に記載されています。

2. Bill is involved in hotel and restaurant (　　　　　).
   ビルはホテルとレストラン経営を手がけている。

3. Fred called a customer service (　　　　　) to complain.
   フレッドは顧客サービス担当者に電話をかけてクレームをつけた。

4. Qualified (　　　　　) must have practical experience in accounting.
   資格のある応募者は経理の実務経験が必要です。

5. Did you confirm the details of the (　　　　　)?
   リフォームの詳細を確認しましたか。

🎧 28

6. Local (　　　　　) provided feedback on the city's website.
   地元住民は市のウェブサイトに意見を提供した。

7. My laptop has some exciting new (　　　　　).
   私のノートパソコンにはわくわくする新しい特徴がいくつかある。

8. The (　　　　　) was returned to the manufacturer.
   その商品はメーカーに返品された。

9. Susie's travel and accommodation (　　　　　) were approved.
   スージーの移動と宿泊にかかった経費は承認された。

10. The board of directors listened to a project (　　　　　).
    取締役会のメンバーたちはプロジェクトの提案に耳を傾けた。

---

| ☐ candidate | ☐ invoice | ☐ proposal | ☐ resident |
| ☐ expense | ☐ management | ☐ renovation | |
| ☐ feature | ☐ merchandise | ☐ representative | |

## 5-C
音声を聴き、英文の空所にあてはまる単語を入れ、その単語に該当する日本語を○で囲みましょう。
（単語は必要に応じて変化させましょう。）

1. The clothing items are made from recycled plastic ( packaging ).
   その衣料品はプラスチック包装材をリサイクルしたものから作られている。

2. The ( development ) of the new vehicle was delayed.
   その新車両の開発は遅れた。

3. Our online store issued a ( refund ) to your account.
   当オンラインストアはお客様の口座に返金をいたしました。

4. Consult the manual if you have a problem with the ( device ).
   装置に関してお困りの場合はマニュアルをご覧ください。

5. Lucy attended the annual ( convention ) with her colleague.
   ルーシーは同僚と年次大会に出席した。

6. We provide immediate ( estimates ) for the cost of facility repairs.
   当社は施設修繕の費用の見積もりをすぐにご提供いたします。

7. The location of the property is near public ( transportation ).
   その不動産物件の場所は公共交通機関に近い。

8. Which message ( app ) do you recommend for mobile phones?
   携帯電話にはどのメッセージアプリがお勧めですか。

9. The supervisor updated the training ( materials ) for new employees.
   上司は新入社員研修用の資料を更新した。

10. The consultant suggested reducing the ( amount ) of inventory.
    コンサルタントは在庫の量を減らすことを提案した。

- [ ] amount
- [ ] development
- [ ] material
- [ ] transportation
- [ ] app
- [ ] device
- [ ] packaging
- [ ] convention
- [ ] estimate
- [ ] refund

## 5-D

● それぞれの語の類義語を、この UNIT の見出し語から選びましょう。

1) characteristic _____
2) conference _____
3) cost _____
4) goods _____
5) restoration _____

● それぞれの語の動詞形を書きましょう。

1) development _____
2) management _____
3) proposal _____
4) representative _____
5) transportation _____

## 5-E

空所に入る最も適切な語を選びましょう。ただし、それぞれの語の意味はこの UNIT で取り扱ったものとします。

1. The successful ------ will have excellent English and Spanish language skills.

    (A) candidate    (B) development    (C) invoice    (D) material

2. They found the manufacturer's new ------ difficult to open.

    (A) feature    (B) packaging    (C) refund    (D) renovation

3. The new recording ------ in our department is actually out of order.

    (A) convention    (B) device    (C) proposal    (D) transportation

4. It took much longer than expected to develop the gaming ------.

    (A) app    (B) estimate    (C) expense    (D) representative

5. You shouldn't have paid the full ------ for the hotel room.

    (A) amount    (B) management    (C) merchandise    (D) resident

# UNIT 6
## 動詞 2

**6-A** それぞれの英単語の意味に最も当てはまる日本語を選びましょう。

🎧31

1) **advertise** [ǽdvərtàɪz] _____

2) **increase** [ɪnkríːs] _____

3) **lead** [líːd] _____

4) **encourage** [ɪnkə́ːrɪdʒ] _____

5) **revise** [rɪváɪz] _____

6) **deliver** [dɪlívər] _____

7) **host** [hóʊst] _____

8) **improve** [ɪmprúːv] _____

9) **mention** [ménʃən] _____

10) **reserve** [rɪzə́ːrv] _____

🎧32

11) **approve** [əprúːv] _____

12) **replace** [rɪpléɪs] _____

13) **install** [ɪnstɔ́ːl] _____

14) **repair** [rɪpéər] _____

15) **feature** [fíːtʃər] _____

16) **participate (in)** [pɑːrtísəpèɪt] _____

17) **apply (for)** [əpláɪ] _____

18) **inform** [ɪnfɔ́ːrm] _____

19) **accept** [əksépt] _____

20) **promote** [prəmóʊt] _____

| | | | |
|---|---|---|---|
| 受け入れる | 改善する | 言及する | 参加する |
| 修正する | 修理する | 主催する | 承認する |
| 奨励する | 知らせる | 設置する | 宣伝広告する |
| 特集する | 取り替える | 取り仕切る | 配達する |
| 販売促進する | 増やす | 申し込む | 予約する |

## 6-B

音声を聴き、英文の空所にあてはまる単語を入れ、その単語に該当する日本語を○で囲みましょう。
（単語は必要に応じて変化させましょう。）

🎧 33

1. What does the speaker (　　　　　　) about the packaging material?
   話し手はその包装材の材料に関してどのようなことに言及していますか。

2. Ellen (　　　　　　) an afternoon session at the convention.
   エレンはその大会で午後のセッションを取り仕切った。

3. The production process in the factory was (　　　　　　).
   その工場の生産工程が改善された。

4. The company (　　　　　　) the budget for development of the new device.
   その会社は新しいデバイスの開発の予算を増やした。

5. Workshop participants are (　　　　　　) to take public transportation.
   講習会の参加者は公共交通機関を利用することが奨励されています。

🎧 34

6. They (　　　　　　) a management seminar at the community center.
   彼らはコミュニティセンターで経営セミナーを主催した。

7. Matt was required to (　　　　　　) the financial document.
   マットは財務に関する文書を修正するよう求められた。

8. Our new product was (　　　　　　) on various apps.
   当社の新製品はさまざまなアプリで宣伝広告された。

9. George (　　　　　　) a meeting room for the job interview.
   ジョージは就職面接のために会議室を予約した。

10. Let me know when the shipment is (　　　　　　).
    発送品が配達されたら知らせてください。

---

| ☐ advertise | ☐ host | ☐ lead | ☐ revise |
| ☐ deliver | ☐ improve | ☐ mention | |
| ☐ encourage | ☐ increase | ☐ reserve | |

## 6-C

音声を聴き、英文の空所にあてはまる単語を入れ、その単語に該当する日本語を○で囲みましょう。
（単語は必要に応じて変化させましょう。）

🎧 35

1. We need to (　　　　　　) our merchandise on social media.
   ソーシャルメディアで当社の商品を販売促進する必要がある。

2. The budget for the advertisement was (　　　　　　).
   その広告の予算は承認された。

3. The fountain was (　　　　　　) at the request of the residents.
   その噴水は住民の要望で修理された。

4. The shop (　　　　　　) customers of its new refund policy.
   その店舗は顧客に新しい返金規定を知らせた。

5. Security cameras are (　　　　　　) at the main entrance.
   監視カメラが正面玄関に設置されている。

🎧 36

6. The sales representative (　　　　　　) a job offer from a competitor.
   その営業担当者は競合会社からの職のオファーを受け入れた。

7. I (　　　　　　) for a position with a shipping company.
   私は配送会社での職に申し込んだ。

8. The maintenance staff (　　　　　　) the light fixtures.
   保守整備スタッフが照明器具を取り替えた。

9. An entry fee is required to (　　　　　　) in the competition.
   その競技会に参加するためには登録料が必要だ。

10. The construction industry leaders were (　　　　　　) in a magazine.
    建設業界のトップの人たちが雑誌で特集された。

---

| ☐ accept | ☐ feature | ☐ participate (in) | ☐ replace |
| ☐ apply (for) | ☐ inform | ☐ promote | |
| ☐ approve | ☐ install | ☐ repair | |

UNIT 6／動詞 2

## 6-D

● それぞれの語の類義語を、このUNITの見出し語から選びましょう。

1) book _____
2) exchange _____
3) mend _____
4) publicize _____
5) receive _____

● それぞれの語の名詞形を書きましょう。

1) approve _____
2) deliver _____
3) improve _____
4) inform _____
5) install _____

## 6-E

空所に入る最も適切な語を選びましょう。ただし、それぞれの語の意味はこのUNITで取り扱ったものとします。

**1.** I'd like to ------ a table for four on the patio at noon.

   (A) advertise   (B) host   (C) mention   (D) reserve

**2.** The museum is planning to ------ sculptures by contemporary artists.

   (A) apply for   (B) feature   (C) improve   (D) revise

**3.** Who will ------ the restoration project of the city's landmark?

   (A) deliver   (B) increase   (C) lead   (D) repair

**4.** I'd like to ------ all employees to attend the company's fund-raising event.

   (A) accept   (B) approve   (C) encourage   (D) promote

**5.** Did you ------ the consumer survey conducted by the bank?

   (A) inform   (B) install   (C) participate in   (D) replace

# UNIT 7
## 名詞 5

**7-A** それぞれの英単語の意味に最も当てはまる日本語を選びましょう。

1) **package** [pǽkɪdʒ]

2) **quarter** [kwɔ́ːrtər]

3) **automobile** [ɔ́ːtəmoʊbìːl]

4) **celebration** [sèləbréɪʃən]

5) **recipe** [résəpi]

6) **trail** [tréɪl]

7) **author** [ɔ́ːθər]

8) **career** [kəríər]

9) **laptop** [lǽptɑ̀p]

10) **manufacturer** [mæ̀njəfǽktʃər]

11) **gallery** [gǽləri]

12) **inspection** [ɪnspékʃən]

13) **line** [láɪn]

14) **assignment** [əsáɪnmənt]

15) **delay** [dɪléɪ]

16) **invitation** [ìnvətéɪʃən]

17) **fair** [féər]

18) **passenger** [pǽsəndʒər]

19) **receipt** [rɪsíːt]

20) **bill** [bíl]

| | | | |
|---|---|---|---|
| 遅れ | 画廊 | 検査 | 自動車 |
| 四半期 | 祝賀（会） | 乗客 | 招待（状） |
| 商品（のタイプ） | 職（歴） | 請求書 | セット商品 |
| 著者 | 登山道 | ノートパソコン | 見本市 |
| メーカー | 領収書 | レシピ | 割り当てられた仕事 |

## 7-B
音声を聴き、英文の空所にあてはまる単語を入れ、その単語に該当する日本語を○で囲みましょう。
（単語は必要に応じて変化させましょう。）

1. The company successfully reduced its operating expenses this ( ).
   その会社はこの四半期に営業経費を削減することに成功した。

2. We were selected from several textile ( ).
   いくつかの織物メーカーから当社が選ばれた。

3. The magazine features ( ) for Italian cuisine.
   その雑誌はイタリア料理のレシピを特集している。

4. There were a lot of vintage ( ) on display at the museum.
   多くのビンテージものの自動車が博物館に展示されていた。

5. The ( ) didn't mention the reviews of her latest book.
   その著者は自分の最新作の批評には言及しなかった。

6. Nancy began her ( ) in the hospitality industry.
   ナンシーは接客業界で彼女の職歴をスタートさせた。

7. The agency promoted the hotel's weekend ( ) which included complimentary meals.
   代理店はそのホテルの無料の食事を含む週末向けのセット商品を販売促進した。

8. The new ( ) was delivered in the small box.
   新しいノートパソコンが小さな箱で届けられた。

9. Mary participated in a hiking tour of the new and improved ( ).
   メアリはその改善された新しい登山道のハイキングツアーに参加した。

10. The mayor hosted a ( ) of the city's 100th anniversary.
    市長は市の100周年の記念日の祝賀会を主催した。

---

- ☐ author
- ☐ celebration
- ☐ package
- ☐ trail
- ☐ automobile
- ☐ laptop
- ☐ quarter
- ☐ career
- ☐ manufacturer
- ☐ recipe

## 7-C
音声を聴き、英文の空所にあてはまる単語を入れ、その単語に該当する日本語を○で囲みましょう。
（単語は必要に応じて変化させましょう。）

🎧 41

1. The ( passengers ) were informed of a change in boarding time.
   乗客は搭乗時間の変更を知らされた。

2. Susie received an incorrect ( bill ) from the vendor.
   スージーは仕入れ業者から間違った請求書を受け取った。

3. We would like to extend an ( invitation ) to you for our annual convention.
   わたくしどもの年次大会にあなた様をご招待させていただきたく存じます。

4. Should I accept or reject the new ( assignment )?
   その新しく割り当てられた仕事を引き受けるべきでしょうか、それとも断るべきでしょうか。

5. An annual safety ( inspection ) of the facility was conducted.
   その施設の年に一度の安全検査が行われた。

🎧 42

6. What caused the ( delay ) in the store renovation?
   店のリフォームの遅れはなぜ起きたのですか。

7. The art ( gallery ) replaced some paintings on display with other ones.
   その美術画廊は展示中の数点の絵画を他のものと取り替えた。

8. Matt found the original ( receipt ) for office supplies.
   マットは事務用品の領収書の原本を見つけた。

9. The company advertised its ( line ) of autumn footwear on television.
   その会社はテレビで秋物の靴の商品を宣伝広告した。

10. They apologized for the last-minute cancellation of the food ( fair ).
    彼らは食の見本市が直前で中止になったことを謝罪した。

---

| ☐ assignment | ☐ fair | ☐ invitation | ☐ receipt |
| --- | --- | --- | --- |
| ☐ bill | ☐ gallery | ☐ line | |
| ☐ delay | ☐ inspection | ☐ passenger | |

## 7-D

● それぞれの語の類義語を、このUNITの見出し語から選びましょう。

1) car　　　_____

2) examination　_____

3) invoice　_____

4) maker　_____

5) path　_____

● それぞれの語の動詞形を書きましょう。

1) assignment　_____

2) celebration　_____

3) invitation　_____

4) package　_____

5) receipt　_____

## 7-E

空所に入る最も適切な語を選びましょう。ただし、それぞれの語の意味はこのUNITで取り扱ったものとします。

1. The agency was encouraged to set up a booth at the travel ------.

    (A) author　　(B) fair　　(C) manufacturer　　(D) package

2. The sales increase in the third ------ was more than the CEO expected.

    (A) delay　　(B) quarter　　(C) receipt　　(D) trail

3. Each ------ is allowed to carry one piece of hand luggage on board.

    (A) career　　(B) inspection　　(C) line　　(D) passenger

4. The ------ for the dish we introduced today is available on our website.

    (A) celebration　　(B) invitation　　(C) laptop　　(D) recipe

5. Our ------ has specialized in works by local artists for years.

    (A) assignment　　(B) automobile　　(C) bill　　(D) gallery

30　第1部

# UNIT 8
## 形容詞 1

**8-A** それぞれの英単語の意味に最も当てはまる日本語を選びましょう。

1) **available** [əvéɪləbl] _____

2) **local** [lóʊkl] _____

3) **additional** [ədíʃənl] _____

4) **online** [á:nlaɪn] _____

5) **financial** [fənǽnʃəl] _____

6) **extra** [ékstrə] _____

7) **annual** [ǽnjuəl] _____

8) **upcoming** [ʌ́pkʌ̀mɪŋ] _____

9) **medical** [médɪkl] _____

10) **concerned** [kənsə́:rnd] _____

11) **corporate** [kɔ́:rpərət] _____

12) **available** [əvéɪləbl] _____

13) **following** [fá:loʊɪŋ] _____

14) **potential** [pəténʃəl] _____

15) **due** [d(j)ú:] _____

16) **electronic** [ɪlèktrá:nɪk] _____

17) **latest** [léɪtɪst] _____

18) **retail** [rí:tèɪl] _____

19) **complimentary** [kà:mpləméntəri] _____

20) **missing** [mísɪŋ] _____

| | | | |
|---|---|---|---|
| 医療の | オンラインの | 会社の | 可能性のある |
| 小売りの | 今度の [まもなく起こる] | 最新の | 財政上の |
| （支払）期限が来た | 地元の | 心配して | 追加の [よりフォーマル] |
| 次の [あとに続く] | 都合がつく | 電子の | 入手できる |
| 毎年の | 無料の | 行方不明の | 余分の [よりカジュアル] |

## 8-B
音声を聴き、英文の空所にあてはまる単語を入れ、その単語に該当する日本語を○で囲みましょう。
（単語は必要に応じて変化させましょう。）

1. The author received an invitation to the ( annual ) book fair.
   その著者は毎年開催のブックフェアへの招待状を受け取った。

2. New equipment was installed at the ( medical ) center.
   新しい機器が医療センターに設置された。

3. The application form is ( available ) at the counter.
   その申込用紙は窓口で入手できる。

4. Who will lead the ( upcoming ) training session?
   誰が今度の講習会を取り仕切りますか。

5. The consultant presented several options to overcome ( financial ) difficulties.
   コンサルタントは財政上の困難を克服するいくつかの選択肢を提示した。

6. ( Online ) reviews indicate that the laptop is excellent.
   オンラインレビューはそのノートパソコンがすぐれていることを示している。

7. What ( additional ) fees were listed on the invoice?
   どのような追加料金が送り状に載っていましたか。

8. Cathy was ( concerned ) about the production delay.
   キャシーは生産の遅れを心配していた。

9. Ray made some ( extra ) copies of the meeting material.
   レイは会議用資料の余分の部数を作った。

10. The auto manufacturer held a reception at the ( local ) hotel.
    その自動車メーカーは地元のホテルで祝賀会を開いた。

---

| ☐ additional | ☐ concerned | ☐ local | ☐ upcoming |
| ☐ annual | ☐ extra | ☐ medical | |
| ☐ available | ☐ financial | ☐ online | |

## 8-C 音声を聴き、英文の空所にあてはまる単語を入れ、その単語に該当する日本語を○で囲みましょう。
（単語は必要に応じて変化させましょう。）

1. The ( ) payroll policy has been revised.
   会社の給与方針が見直された。

2. The file containing the images is ( ).
   画像の入っているファイルが行方不明だ。

3. Passengers turned off their ( ) devices during takeoff.
   乗客は離陸時に電子機器の電源を切った。

4. The ads for our line of footwear should attract ( ) customers.
   その当社の靴製品の広告は顧客になる可能性のある人たちを引き付けるはずだ。

5. Our products are sold at certain ( ) locations.
   当社の製品は一部の小売店舗で販売されている。

6. The artist wasn't ( ) to meet with the gallery owner.
   その芸術家は画廊のオーナーと会う都合がつかなかった。

7. The tour package includes ( ) breakfast.
   そのパック旅行には無料の朝食が含まれています。

8. The budget proposal for the next quarter is ( ) tomorrow.
   次の四半期の予算案は明日提出期限が来る。

9. The ( ) items were approved at the board meeting.
   次の事項が役員会で承認された。

10. Emily purchased the chef's ( ) recipe book.
    エミリーはそのシェフの最新のレシピ本を購入した。

---

☐ available   ☐ due         ☐ latest     ☐ retail
☐ complimentary ☐ electronic ☐ missing
☐ corporate   ☐ following   ☐ potential

## 8-D

- それぞれの語の類義語を、このUNITの見出し語から選びましょう。

1) additional _____
2) anxious _____
3) lost _____
4) possible _____
5) yearly _____

- それぞれの語の名詞形を書きましょう。

1) additional _____
2) available _____
3) corporate _____
4) financial _____
5) medical _____

## 8-E

空所に入る最も適切な語を選びましょう。ただし、それぞれの語の意味はこのUNITで取り扱ったものとします。

1. Tom was not ------ to deliver the keynote speech at the conference.

    (A) available　　(B) extra　　(C) online　　(D) upcoming

2. The payment of the monthly subscription fee is ------ today.

    (A) additional　　(B) concerned　　(C) due　　(D) potential

3. In which of the four positions does the ------ sentence best belong?

    (A) complimentary　　(B) electronic　　(C) following　　(D) local

4. The vendor distributes a variety of merchandise to ------ stores.

    (A) annual　　(B) latest　　(C) missing　　(D) retail

5. Are there any business class seats ------ on the flight to Hawaii?

    (A) available　　(B) corporate　　(C) financial　　(D) medical

# UNIT 9
## 名詞6

**9-A** それぞれの英単語の意味に最も当てはまる日本語を選びましょう。

1) **brochure** [bróuʃúər] _____

2) **instructions** [ɪnstrʌ́kʃənz] _____

3) **inventory** [ínvəntɔ̀:ri] _____

4) **account** [əkáunt] _____

5) **editor** [édətər] _____

6) **storage** [stɔ́:rɪdʒ] _____

7) **traffic** [trǽfɪk] _____

8) **warehouse** [wéərhàus] _____

9) **banquet** [bǽŋkwət] _____

10) **catering** [kéɪtərɪŋ] _____

11) **charge** [tʃá:rdʒ] _____

12) **performance** [pərfɔ́:rməns] _____

13) **promotion** [prəmóuʃən] _____

14) **registration** [rèdʒəstréɪʃən] _____

15) **résumé** [rézəmèɪ] _____

16) **task** [tǽsk] _____

17) **branch** [brǽntʃ] _____

18) **patient** [péɪʃənt] _____

19) **procedure** [prəsí:dʒər] _____

20) **suggestion** [səgdʒéstʃən] _____

| | | | |
|---|---|---|---|
| 宴会 | 患者 | ケータリング（業） | 公演 |
| 口座 | 在庫 | 支店 | 昇進 |
| 使用説明書 | 倉庫 | 通行（量） | 提案 |
| 手続き | 登録 | 任務 | パンフレット |
| 編集者 | 保管 | 料金 | 履歴書 |

## 9-B 音声を聴き、英文の空所にあてはまる単語を入れ、その単語に該当する日本語を〇で囲みましょう。
(単語は必要に応じて変化させましょう。)

1. Jim is the ( editor ) of a medical journal.
   ジムは医学専門誌の編集者だ。

2. Why don't we produce a promotional ( brochure )?
   販売促進用のパンフレットを作成しましょう。

3. Some form of identification is required to open a bank ( account ).
   銀行口座を開設するには何か身分証明書が必要だ。

4. Who'll arrange hotel ( catering ) for the upcoming party?
   誰が今度のパーティーのためのホテルのケータリングの手はずを整えるのですか。

5. Visitor ( traffic ) in the amusement park is monitored.
   遊園地内の来場者の通行は監視されている。

6. The facility has extra space for food ( storage ).
   その施設には食料保管用の追加のスペースがある。

7. Employees are encouraged to attend the company's annual ( banquet ).
   従業員は会社の年に一度の宴会に出席することを奨励されている。

8. The retail shop is concerned about its large ( inventory ).
   その小売店は在庫が多いことを気にかけている。

9. A surprise inspection of the ( warehouse ) was conducted.
   倉庫の抜き打ち検査が行われた。

10. Be sure to read the ( instructions ) before assembling the shelf.
    その棚を組み立てる前に必ず使用説明書をお読みください。

---

| ☐ account | ☐ catering | ☐ inventory | ☐ warehouse |
| ☐ banquet | ☐ editor | ☐ storage | |
| ☐ brochure | ☐ instructions | ☐ traffic | |

## 9-C

音声を聴き、英文の空所にあてはまる単語を入れ、その単語に該当する日本語を◯で囲みましょう。
（単語は必要に応じて変化させましょう。）

1. The additional shipping ( ) for the item is $10.
   その商品の追加の配送料は 10 ドルになります。

2. Our next ( ) is to find a potential supplier.
   われわれの次の任務は契約の可能性のある供給業者を見つけることだ。

3. The company reviewed the ( ) for submitting receipts.
   その会社は領収書の提出の手続きを見直した。

4. Jack reserved a seat for the musical ( ).
   ジャックはミュージカル公演の席を予約した。

5. Laura began her banking career at a local ( ).
   ローラは地元の支店から彼女の銀行業の職歴をスタートさせた。

6. The general hospital sent a bill to the ( ).
   その総合病院はその患者に請求書を送った。

7. Online ( ) for the convention is still available.
   その大会のオンライン登録はまだできる。

8. Email your ( ) to our human resources department.
   貴殿の履歴書を当社の人事部へメールでお送りください。

9. Kate applied for a ( ) to senior financial analyst.
   ケイトは上級財政アナリストへの昇進を申請した。

10. James made ( ) for improving corporate governance.
    ジェイムズはコーポレートガバナンスを改善する提案をした。

---

| ☐ branch | ☐ performance | ☐ registration | ☐ task |
| ☐ charge | ☐ procedure | ☐ résumé | |
| ☐ patient | ☐ promotion | ☐ suggestion | |

## 9-D

● それぞれの語の類義語を、このUNITの見出し語から選びましょう。

1) CV _____
2) pamphlet _____
3) proposal _____
4) show _____
5) stock _____

● それぞれの語の動詞形を書きましょう。

1) editor _____
2) instructions _____
3) promotion _____
4) registration _____
5) storage _____

## 9-E

空所に入る最も適切な語を選びましょう。ただし、それぞれの語の意味はこのUNITで取り扱ったものとします。

1. The new shopping mall caused a significant increase in holiday ------.

    (A) brochure　　(B) procedure　　(C) registration　　(D) traffic

2. The restaurant did the ------ for the company's 50th anniversary celebration.

    (A) account　　(B) catering　　(C) instructions　　(D) storage

3. We offer same-day delivery to our members at no extra ------.

    (A) charge　　(B) performance　　(C) suggestion　　(D) warehouse

4. The supervisor helped her subordinates to complete the complex ------.

    (A) banquet　　(B) editor　　(C) patient　　(D) task

5. The clothing company is planning to open its first overseas ------.

    (A) branch　　(B) inventory　　(C) promotion　　(D) résumé

# UNIT 10
## 動詞 3

**10-A** それぞれの英単語の意味に最も当てはまる日本語を選びましょう。

1) **arrange** [əréɪndʒ] _____
2) **remove** [rɪmúːv] _____
3) **extend** [ɪksténd] _____
4) **register (for)** [rédʒɪstər] _____
5) **attract** [ətrǽkt] _____
6) **expand** [ɪkspǽnd] _____
7) **book** [búk] _____
8) **remind** [rɪmáɪnd] _____
9) **suggest** [səgdʒést] _____
10) **organize** [ɔ́ːrɡənàɪz] _____

11) **rent** [rént] _____
12) **post** [póʊst] _____
13) **delay** [dɪléɪ] _____
14) **meet** [míːt] _____
15) **win** [wín] _____
16) **develop** [dɪvéləp] _____
17) **contain** [kəntéɪn] _____
18) **fix** [fíks] _____
19) **publish** [pʌ́blɪʃ] _____
20) **renovate** [rénəvèɪt] _____

| | | | |
|---|---|---|---|
| 暗に示す | 延長する [線を伸ばす] | 遅らせる | 思い出させる |
| 開発する | 拡大する [面を広げる] | 獲得する | 掲示する |
| 修理する | 出版する | 準備する [十分に計画する] | 賃貸借する |
| 手はずを整える [事前に手配する] | 含む | 登録する | 取り外す |
| 引き付ける | | 満たす | 予約する |
| リフォームする | | | |

## 10-B

音声を聴き、英文の空所にあてはまる単語を入れ、その単語に該当する日本語を○で囲みましょう。
（単語は必要に応じて変化させましょう。）

1. The restaurant ( expanded ) its catering service area.
   そのレストランはケータリングサービスのエリアを拡大した。

2. Fred decided to ( register ) for the training session.
   フレッドはその講習会に登録することに決めた。

3. Our branch manager was in charge of ( organizing ) the company's charity event.
   われわれの支店長が社のチャリティーイベントを準備する責任者だった。

4. The poster for the dance performance was ( removed ).
   そのダンス公演のポスターが取り外された。

5. Mike ( reminded ) his colleagues about their year-end banquet.
   マイクは同僚たちに自分たちの忘年会のことを思い出させた。

6. The editor ( arranged ) a conference call with the writer.
   編集者はその作家との電話会議の手はずを整えた。

7. The beautiful nature trails ( attract ) hikers to the national park.
   美しい自然遊歩道がその国立公園にハイキング客を引き付ける。

8. What is ( suggested ) about the construction project?
   建設計画についてどのようなことが暗に示されていますか。

9. The deadline for submission of résumés was ( extended ).
   履歴書の提出の締め切りが延長された。

10. Anne ( booked ) a flight for the following day.
    アンはその次の日のフライトを予約した。

---

- [ ] arrange
- [ ] expand
- [ ] register (for)
- [ ] suggest
- [ ] attract
- [ ] extend
- [ ] remind
- [ ] book
- [ ] organize
- [ ] remove

## 10-C

音声を聴き、英文の空所にあてはまる単語を入れ、その単語に該当する日本語を○で囲みましょう。
（単語は必要に応じて変化させましょう。）

1. The instructions for the refrigerator ( ) some errors.
   その冷蔵庫の使用説明書はいくつかミスプリントを含んでいる。

2. Electronic travel brochures are ( ) on our website.
   旅行の電子パンフレットは当社のウェブサイトに掲示されております。

3. Our warehouse is being ( ) next week.
   当社の倉庫は来週リフォームされることになっている。

4. We ( ) an industry award for our latest laptop.
   当社の最新のノートパソコンで業界の賞を獲得した。

5. Bill's work assignment today is to ( ) some copiers.
   ビルの今日の仕事の割り当ては何台かのコピー機を修理することだ。

6. Matt ( ) storage space in order to increase the amount of inventory.
   マットは在庫量を増やすために保管スペースを賃借した。

7. When will the special issue of the magazine be ( )?
   その雑誌の特別号はいつ出版されますか。

8. That hospital will ( ) the patients' needs.
   その病院は患者たちのニーズを満たすだろう。

9. Shipments were temporarily ( ) because of the power outrage.
   停電のせいで発送が一時的に遅れた。

10. Lucy's task was to ( ) the company's first mobile app.
    ルーシーの任務は会社初の携帯電話用のアプリを開発することだった。

| ☐ contain | ☐ fix | ☐ publish | ☐ win |
| ☐ delay | ☐ meet | ☐ renovate | |
| ☐ develop | ☐ post | ☐ rent | |

## 10-D

● それぞれの語の類義語を、この UNIT の見出し語から選びましょう。

1) fulfill _____
2) gain _____
3) include _____
4) lease _____
5) reserve _____

● それぞれの語の名詞形を書きましょう。

1) arrange _____
2) attract _____
3) develop _____
4) extend _____
5) renovate _____

## 10-E

空所に入る最も適切な語を選びましょう。ただし、それぞれの語の意味はこの UNIT で取り扱ったものとします。

1. Anyone is allowed to ------ comments on the message board of our website.

   (A) book       (B) develop      (C) extend      (D) post

2. Ellen had a local plumber ------ the tap in the kitchen.

   (A) attract    (B) contain      (C) fix         (D) organize

3. David tried to ------ the packing material from the goods that had been delivered.

   (A) delay      (B) meet         (C) publish     (D) remove

4. Sally was supposed to ------ a cooking competition held the following week.

   (A) register for  (B) renovate   (C) rent        (D) suggest

5. Let me ------ you that your sales reports are due by noon.

   (A) arrange    (B) expand       (C) remind      (D) win

# UNIT 11
## 名詞 7

**11-A** それぞれの英単語の意味に最も当てはまる日本語を選びましょう。

1) **warranty** [wɔ́(ː)rənti] _____

2) **appliance** [əpláɪəns] _____

3) **assistance** [əsístəns] _____

4) **beverage** [bévərɪdʒ] _____

5) **confirmation** [kɑ̀ːnfərméɪʃən] _____

6) **finance** [fáɪnæns] _____

7) **image** [ímɪdʒ] _____

8) **laboratory [lab]** [lǽbərətɔ̀ːri] _____

9) **luggage** [lʌ́ɡɪdʒ] _____

10) **anniversary** [æ̀nəvə́ːrsəri] _____

11) **council** [káʊnsl] _____

12) **coworker** [kóʊwə̀ːrkər] _____

13) **electronics** [ɪlèktrάːnɪks] _____

14) **merger** [mə́ːrdʒər] _____

15) **replacement** [rɪpléɪsmənt] _____

16) **update** [ʌ́pdèɪt] _____

17) **agreement** [əɡríːmənt] _____

18) **donation** [doʊnéɪʃən] _____

19) **exhibition** [èksəbíʃən] _____

20) **expert** [ékspəːrt] _____

---

| | | | |
|---|---|---|---|
| 援助 | 確認 | 画像 | 合併 |
| 代わり（の物・人） | 記念日 | 寄付 | 契約（書） |
| 研究所 | 最新情報 | 財務 | 専門家 |
| 手荷物類 | 電化製品 | 展示会 | 電子機器 |
| 同僚 | 飲み物 | 評議会 | 保証 |

## 11-B 音声を聴き、英文の空所にあてはまる単語を入れ、その単語に該当する日本語を○で囲みましょう。
（単語は必要に応じて変化させましょう。）

1. The extended ( ) enabled me to get my fridge repaired for free.
   延長保証のおかげで私は冷蔵庫を無料で修理してもらえた。

2. Complimentary ( ) were served at the convention.
   その大会では無料の飲み物が出された。

3. The suitcase is the standard size for carry-on ( ).
   そのスーツケースは機内持ち込み手荷物類の基準のサイズだ。

4. John got ( ) of his registration for the workshop by email.
   ジョンはメールでその講習会の登録の確認を得た。

5. Our website contains ( ) that are available at no charge.
   当ウェブサイトは無料でご利用できる画像を含んでおります。

6. I asked for George's ( ) in organizing Linda's promotion party.
   私はリンダの昇進パーティーを準備するのにジョージの援助を求めた。

7. Ray arranged to celebrate his shop's fifth ( ).
   レイは自分の店の5周年記念日を祝う手はずを整えた。

8. The ( ) posted a job opening on its website.
   その研究所はウェブサイトに求人を掲載した。

9. The best feature of this kitchen ( ) is that it is energy-efficient.
   この台所用電化製品の最大の特徴はエネルギー効率が良いことだ。

10. Mary was promoted to vice president of ( ).
    メアリは財務担当副社長に昇進した。

---

☐ anniversary　☐ beverage　☐ image　☐ warranty
☐ appliance　☐ confirmation　☐ laboratory
☐ assistance　☐ finance　☐ luggage

## 11-C

音声を聴き、英文の空所にあてはまる単語を入れ、その単語に該当する日本語を○で囲みましょう。
（単語は必要に応じて変化させましょう。）

1. The city ( council ) decided to extend the present session.
   市議会は現在の会期を延長することを決定した。

2. Jane said that she was available to visit the product ( exhibition ).
   ジェインはその製品展示会を訪れる都合がついたと言った。

3. The CEO delayed the announcement of the ( merger ).
   その CEO は合併の発表を遅らせた。

4. My ( coworker ) won a prize in the sales competition.
   私の同僚はその売上コンテストで賞を獲得した。

5. The lawyer signed an ( agreement ) to rent her office.
   その弁護士は自分のオフィスを賃借するために契約書にサインをした。

6. The culinary ( expert ) published a recipe book.
   その料理専門家はレシピ本を出版した。

7. Our company is involved in manufacturing ( electronics ).
   当社は電子機器を製造することに従事している。

8. Nancy turned on the car radio for traffic ( updates ).
   ナンシーは交通の最新情報を得るためにカーラジオをつけた。

9. We will send you a ( replacement ) right away.
   お客様にはすぐに代わりの品をお送りさせていただきます。

10. The museum was renovated using large ( donations ) from some local companies.
    その美術館はいくつかの地元企業からの多くの寄付でリフォームされた。

---

- [ ] agreement
- [ ] donation
- [ ] expert
- [ ] update
- [ ] council
- [ ] electronics
- [ ] merger
- [ ] coworker
- [ ] exhibition
- [ ] replacement

## 11-D

● それぞれの語の類義語を、このUNITの見出し語から選びましょう。

1) baggage _____
2) colleague _____
3) contract _____
4) drink _____
5) guarantee _____

● それぞれの語の動詞形を書きましょう。

1) assistance _____
2) confirmation _____
3) donation _____
4) exhibition _____
5) merger _____

## 11-E

空所に入る最も適切な語を選びましょう。ただし、それぞれの語の意味はこのUNITで取り扱ったものとします。

1. The local ------ unanimously approved plans for the subway extension.

    (A) appliance    (B) council    (C) exhibition    (D) update

2. We need a temporary ------ for an employee who is scheduled to take a long vacation.

    (A) anniversary    (B) finance    (C) luggage    (D) replacement

3. The fitness ------ demonstrated how to use the new exercise equipment.

    (A) assistance    (B) beverage    (C) electronics    (D) expert

4. The photographer uploads a high-quality ------ to his online gallery every day.

    (A) coworker    (B) donation    (C) image    (D) warranty

5. The professor gave us a tour of the ------ before we interviewed her.

    (A) agreement    (B) confirmation    (C) laboratory    (D) merger

# UNIT 12
## 動詞 4

**12-A** それぞれの英単語の意味に最も当てはまる日本語を選びましょう。

🎧 67

1) **reschedule** [riːskédʒuːl]

2) **correct** [kərékt]

3) **ensure** [ɪnʃʊ́ər]

4) **own** [óʊn]

5) **propose** [prəpóʊz]

6) **process** [prɑ́ːses]

7) **respond (to)** [rɪspɑ́ːnd]

8) **assign** [əsáɪn]

9) **charge** [tʃɑ́ːrdʒ]

10) **present** [prɪzént]

🎧 68

11) **produce** [prəd(j)úːs]

12) **ship** [ʃíp]

13) **manage** [mǽnɪdʒ]

14) **specialize (in)** [spéʃəlàɪz]

15) **distribute** [dɪstríbjuːt]

16) **inquire (about)** [ɪnkwáɪər]

17) **obtain** [əbtéɪn]

18) **miss** [mís]

19) **recruit** [rɪkrúːt]

20) **adjust** [ədʒʌ́st]

| | | | |
|---|---|---|---|
| 得る | 確実にする | 管理運営する | 所有する |
| 処理する | 新規採用する | 請求する | 製造する |
| 専門に扱う | 対応する | 調整する | 提案する［話を持ち出す］ |
| 提示する［目の前に見せる］ | 訂正する | 問い合わせる | 日程を変更する |
| のがす | 配布する | 発送する | 割り当てる |

## 12-B

音声を聴き、英文の空所にあてはまる単語を入れ、その単語に該当する日本語を○で囲みましょう。
（単語は必要に応じて変化させましょう。）

1. Restricting admission ( ensured ) the security of visitors at the exhibition.
   入場を制限することがその展覧会で入場者の安全を確実にした。

2. I was ( charged ) $10 extra for a five-year warranty.
   5年保証の代金として10ドルの追加料金を請求された。

3. Matt ( owns ) a home electronics store in the city.
   マットはその市で家電店を所有している。

4. Tom ( responded ) to an inquiry about missing luggage.
   トムは行方不明の手荷物の問い合わせに対応した。

5. Emily was ( assigned ) the task of drafting the merger agreement.
   エミリーは合併の協定書を作成するという任務を割り当てられた。

6. Please remind me to ( reschedule ) my visit to the laboratory.
   研究所への訪問の日程を変更することを私にリマインドしてください。

7. The council member ( presented ) plans to rebuild the city's finances.
   その市議会のメンバーは市の財政を再建する計画を提示した。

8. Cathy ( proposed ) offering free technical assistance to some academic labs.
   キャシーはいくつかの大学の研究室に無料で技術支援をすることを提案した。

9. We will ( process ) your request for a replacement battery.
   わたくしどもは代替のバッテリーでお客様のご要望を処理させていただきます。

10. The airline ( corrected ) the information on ticketing procedures.
    その航空会社は発券手続きに関する情報を訂正した。

---

☐ assign    ☐ ensure    ☐ process    ☐ respond (to)
☐ charge    ☐ own       ☐ propose
☐ correct   ☐ present   ☐ reschedule

## 12-C

音声を聴き、英文の空所にあてはまる単語を入れ、その単語に該当する日本語を○で囲みましょう。
（単語は必要に応じて変化させましょう。）

🎧 71

1. Jim ( inquired ) about the due date of the subscription.
   ジムはそのサブスクの支払期限日について問い合わせた。

2. The fuel-efficient cars we ( produce ) have attracted a lot of customers.
   当社が製造する燃料効率の良い車は多くの顧客を引き付けてきた。

3. Laura ( adjusted ) her schedule so that she could attend the anniversary celebration.
   ローラはその記念式典に出席できるようにスケジュールを調整した。

4. Our company ( specializes ) in women's apparel.
   わたくしどもの会社は婦人もの衣料品を専門に扱っております。

5. The handouts my coworker prepared were ( distributed ) at the meeting.
   同僚が作成したハンドアウトが会議で配布された。

🎧 72

6. This software helps you to ( manage ) your website easily.
   このソフトウェアがあればお客さまはご自身のウェブサイトを簡単に管理運営できます。

7. Jack ( missed ) the chance to register for the training session.
   ジャックはその講習会の登録をする機会をのがした。

8. The goods you ordered were ( shipped ) today.
   ご注文の商品は本日発送されました。

9. A new sales manager was ( recruited ) from outside the firm.
   新しい営業部長が社外から新規採用された。

10. Kate ( obtained ) permission from the photographer to use the image.
    ケイトは画像を使う許可をその写真家から得た。

---

| ☐ adjust | ☐ manage | ☐ produce | ☐ specialize (in) |
| ☐ distribute | ☐ miss | ☐ recruit | |
| ☐ inquire (about) | ☐ obtain | ☐ ship | |

## 12-D

● それぞれの語の類義語を、このUNITの見出し語から選びましょう。

1) answer _____
2) ask _____
3) get _____
4) hire _____
5) show _____

● それぞれの語の名詞形を書きましょう。

1) assign _____
2) correct _____
3) distribute _____
4) manage _____
5) propose _____

## 12-E

空所に入る最も適切な語を選びましょう。ただし、それぞれの語の意味はこのUNITで取り扱ったものとします。

1. The president decided to ------ the company event for the following month.

    (A) assign    (B) distribute    (C) obtain    (D) reschedule

2. I had to ------ a large number of online orders from retailers.

    (A) own    (B) process    (C) propose    (D) recruit

3. After the trial period of 30 days, we will begin to ------ subscribers $20 per month.

    (A) adjust    (B) charge    (C) present    (D) respond to

4. If you should ------ the flight, call the client as soon as you can.

    (A) manage    (B) miss    (C) produce    (D) specialize in

5. Our travel packages ------ a great experience for customers of all ages.

    (A) correct    (B) ensure    (C) inquire about    (D) ship

# UNIT 13
## 名詞 8

**13-A** それぞれの英単語の意味に最も当てはまる日本語を選びましょう。

🎧73

1) **memo** [mémoʊ] _____
2) **paperwork** [péɪpərwə̀ːrk] _____
3) **account** [əkáʊnt] _____
4) **attendee** [ətèndíː] _____
5) **board** [bɔ́ːrd] _____
6) **competitor** [kəmpétətər] _____
7) **complaint** [kəmpléɪnt] _____
8) **expo [exposition]** [ékspoʊ] _____
9) **headquarters** [hédkɔ̀ːrtərz] _____
10) **rate** [réɪt] _____

🎧74

11) **response** [rɪspáːns] _____
12) **agenda** [ədʒéndə] _____
13) **agent** [éɪdʒənt] _____
14) **description** [dɪskrípʃən] _____
15) **improvement** [ɪmprúːvmənt] _____
16) **management** [mǽnɪdʒmənt] _____
17) **benefits** [bénəfɪts] _____
18) **competition** [kàːmpətíʃən] _____
19) **crew** [krúː] _____
20) **ingredient** [ɪngríːdiənt] _____

---

| | | | |
|---|---|---|---|
| アカウント | 改善 | 議題 | 競合相手 |
| クレーム | 経営陣 | コンテスト | 材料 |
| 事務書類 | 社内回覧文書 | 出席者 | 説明 |
| 代行業者 | チーム | 手当 | 博覧会 |
| 返答 | 本社 | 役員（会） | 料金 |

## 13-B
音声を聴き、英文の空所にあてはまる単語を入れ、その単語に該当する日本語を○で囲みましょう。
(単語は必要に応じて変化させましょう。)

1. The relocation of our corporate (                ) ensured our success.
   本社の移転がわれわれの成功を確実にした。

2. Lucy responded to customer questions and (                ).
   ルーシーは顧客からの質問とクレームに対応した。

3. The solution that Anne proposed was approved by the (                ).
   アンが提案した解決策が役員に承認された。

4. James was assigned the task of filing the (                ).
   ジェイムズは事務書類を整理保存する任務を割り当てられた。

5. I missed the technology (                ) held last month.
   先月開催された技術博覧会を見逃した。

6. Updates on the project were outlined in the (                ).
   そのプロジェクトの最新情報が社内回覧文書で概説されていた。

7. Many of the conference (                ) booked the same flight.
   その会議の参加者の多くは同じフライトを予約した。

8. We've produced more durable devices than our (                ).
   当社は競合相手よりも耐久性のある機器を製造してきた。

9. Fred created an (                ) for the online store.
   フレッドはそのネットショップのアカウントを作成した。

10. Orders will be shipped at a flat (                ) of $10.
    ご注文品は一律10ドルの料金で配送されます。

---

| ☐ account | ☐ competitor | ☐ headquarters | ☐ rate |
| ☐ attendee | ☐ complaint | ☐ memo | |
| ☐ board | ☐ expo | ☐ paperwork | |

## 13-C

音声を聴き、英文の空所にあてはまる単語を入れ、その単語に該当する日本語を○で囲みましょう。
（単語は必要に応じて変化させましょう。）

🎧77

1. The maintenance (　　　　　) removed the air conditioner in order to fix it.
   保守整備チームは修理するためにエアコンを取り外した。

2. The (　　　　　) determined to reschedule the shareholders' meeting.
   経営陣は株主総会の日程を変更することを決定した。

3. We've made various (　　　　　) to the software.
   われわれはそのソフトウェアにはさまざまな改善を行った。

4. Mike processed the data of the survey (　　　　　) using his computer.
   マイクはコンピュータでアンケート調査の返答のデータを処理した。

5. What is suggested about the cooking (　　　　　)?
   その料理コンテストについてどのようなことが示唆されていますか。

🎧78

6. Susie read the course (　　　　　) carefully before registering for it.
   スージーは登録する前にその講座の説明をよく読んだ。

7. Our restaurant uses the freshest local (　　　　　).
   当レストランは地元のとても新鮮な材料を使っております。

8. I'm calling to inquire about unemployment (　　　　　).
   失業手当について問い合わせるために電話をかけています。

9. The real estate (　　　　　) owns quite a few properties.
   その不動産代理業者はかなり多くの物件を所有している。

10. The meeting (　　　　　) included final confirmation of the company event.
    会議の議題は社のイベントの最終確認を含んでいた。

---

☐ agenda　　☐ competition　　☐ improvement　　☐ response
☐ agent　　　☐ crew　　　　　☐ ingredient　　☐
☐ benefits　　☐ description　　☐ management

UNIT 13／名詞8　53

## 13-D

● それぞれの語の類義語を、このUNITの見出し語から選びましょう。

1) charge _____
2) contest _____
3) feedback _____
4) rival _____
5) team _____

● それぞれの語の動詞形を書きましょう。

1) attendee _____
2) complaint _____
3) description _____
4) improvement _____
5) management _____

## 13-E

空所に入る最も適切な語を選びましょう。ただし、それぞれの語の意味はこのUNITで取り扱ったものとします。

1. We provide our employees with a reasonable salary and excellent ------.

    (A) account    (B) attendee    (C) benefits    (D) complaint

2. The ------ discussed the three plans and voted on the best one.

    (A) board    (B) description    (C) improvement    (D) response

3. The ------ will take place in Kyoto from July 1 to September 30.

    (A) agent    (B) crew    (C) expo    (D) management

4. The last item on the ------ is the release date of our new vehicle.

    (A) agenda    (B) competition    (C) ingredient    (D) rate

5. We plan to have a summer internship at our ------.

    (A) competitor    (B) headquarters    (C) memo    (D) paperwork

# UNIT 14
## 定型表現

**14-A** それぞれの英語表現の意味に最も当てはまる日本語を選びましょう。

🎧79
1) **human resources** _____
2) **real estate** _____
3) **contact information** _____
4) **trade show** _____
5) **grocery store** _____
6) **board of directors** _____
7) **employment agency** _____
8) **conference call** _____
9) **press conference** _____
10) **botanical garden** _____

🎧80
11) **city hall** _____
12) **assembly line** _____
13) **sales figures** _____
14) **baggage claim** _____
15) **box office** _____
16) **bulletin board** _____
17) **public relations** _____
18) **gift certificate** _____
19) **press release** _____
20) **quality control** _____

| | | | |
|---|---|---|---|
| 売上高 | 記者会見 | 組み立てライン | 掲示板 |
| 広報 | 市役所 | 商品券 | 職業紹介所 |
| 植物園 | 食料雑貨店 | 人事部 | チケット売り場 |
| 手荷物受取所 | 電話会議 | 取締役会 | 品質管理 |
| 不動産 | 報道機関向け公式発表 | 見本市 | 連絡先 |

## 14-B 音声を聴き、英文の空欄にあてはまる語句を入れ、その語句に該当する日本語を○で囲みましょう。
（語句中の単語は必要に応じて変化させましょう。）

1. Ellen prepared some equipment for the (                    ).
   エレンは電話会議のために機器の準備をした。

2. The (                    ) considered each item on the agenda.
   取締役会は議題のそれぞれの項目をじっくりと検討した。

3. The agency recommended investing in (                    ).
   その代理店は不動産に投資することを勧めた。

4. We manage the (                    ) under contract to the city.
   わたくしどもは市との契約のもとで植物園を管理運営いたしております。

5. The director of (                    ) attended the board meeting.
   人事部の部長が役員会議に出席した。

6. I entered my (                    ) to create an account.
   私はアカウントを作成するために自分の連絡先を入力した。

7. Matt purchased the ingredients for dinner at the (                    ).
   マットはその食料雑貨店で夕食の材料を購入した。

8. Promotional materials were distributed at the (                    ).
   記者会見では販売促進用の資料が配付された。

9. Our competitor made a presentation at the (                    ).
   当社の競合相手がその見本市でプレゼンをした。

10. Bill filled out some paperwork at the (                    ).
    ビルは職業紹介所で事務書類に必要事項を記入した。

---

☐ board of directors　☐ contact information　☐ human resources
☐ botanical garden　☐ employment agency　☐ press conference
☐ conference call　☐ grocery store　☐ real estate　☐ trade show

## 14-C

音声を聴き、英文の空所にあてはまる語句を入れ、その語句に該当する日本語を○で囲みましょう。
（語句中の単語は必要に応じて変化させましょう。）

1. The awards ceremony for the sports competition was held at the ( ).
   そのスポーツ競技会の表彰式は市役所で行われた。

2. The company immediately corrected the mistake in the ( ).
   その会社は報道機関向け公式発表の誤りをすぐに訂正した。

3. There was a long line at the theater ( ).
   その劇場のチケット売り場には長い列ができていた。

4. The survey respondents received a $10 ( ).
   その調査の回答者は10ドルの商品券を受け取った。

5. Susie waited for her suitcase at ( ) for about an hour.
   スージーは1時間ほど手荷物受取所でスーツケースが出てくるのを待った。

6. The shop owner presented the ( ) to the consultant.
   店のオーナーはコンサルタントに売上高を示した。

7. Ray is in charge of ( ) at the university.
   レイは大学で広報の担当だ。

8. The manufacturer recruited an expert in ( ).
   そのメーカーは品質管理のエキスパートを新規採用した。

9. The management's response was posted on the ( ).
   経営陣の回答が掲示板に張り出された。

10. Workers on the ( ) received special benefits.
    組み立てラインで働いている人たちは特別手当を受け取った。

---

☐ assembly line　☐ bulletin board　☐ press release　☐ sales figures
☐ baggage claim　☐ city hall　☐ public relations
☐ box office　☐ gift certificate　☐ quality control

## 14-D

● それぞれの定型表現の類義表現になるように、指定された出だしの文字で始まる1語を空所に書き込みましょう。

1) human resources   p_____
2) real estate       p_____
3) trade show        trade f_____
4) conference call   p_____ conference
5) press conference  n_____ conference
6) city hall         city o_____
7) box office        t_____ office
8) bulletin board    n_____ board
9) public relations  p_____
10) gift certificate gift v_____

## 14-E

空所に入る最も適切な語句を選びましょう。ただし、それぞれの語句の意味はこの UNIT で取り扱ったものとします。

**1.** George applied for unemployment benefits at the ------.
   (A) box office
   (B) bulletin board
   (C) employment agency
   (D) press release

**2.** Linda exchanged ------ with the keynote speaker at the convention.
   (A) contact information
   (B) grocery store
   (C) press conference
   (D) real estate

**3.** The city has a historic ------ next to the zoo.
   (A) board of directors
   (B) botanical garden
   (C) conference call
   (D) quality control

**4.** John carefully analyzed the firm's ------ in order to offer proper advice.
   (A) baggage claim
   (B) city hall
   (C) gift certificate
   (D) sales figures

**5.** They regularly inspect the equipment on the ------.
   (A) assembly line
   (B) human resources
   (C) public relations
   (D) trade show

# UNIT 15
## 熟語・構文 1

**15-A** それぞれの英熟語・英語構文の意味に最も当てはまる日本語を選びましょう。

1) pick up

2) be located (in / on / etc)

3) set up

4) make sure that 節／be sure to 不定詞

5) sign up (for)

6) work on

7) fill out

8) in advance

9) on time

10) place an order (for)

11) be intended for

12) be supposed to 不定詞

13) in stock

14) due to 名詞

15) be willing to 不定詞

16) stop by

17) be familiar with

18) up to 名詞

19) be in charge of

20) given 名詞 / that 節

---

| | | | |
|---|---|---|---|
| 位置している | 必ず…してください | 快く…する | 在庫があって |
| （最大で）…まで | 参加登録する | 時間通りに | …することになっている |
| セッティングする | 立ち寄る | 注文する | 取り組む |
| 取りに行く[物を]／車で迎えに行く[人を] | 必要事項を記入する | …にくわしい | …のせいで |
| …の担当である | | 前もって | …向けである |
| …を考慮すると | | | |

## 15-B
音声を聴き、英文の空欄にあてはまる語句を入れ、その語句に該当する日本語を○で囲みましょう。
（語句中の単語は必要に応じて変化させましょう。）

1. The venue for the expo (　　　　　　　) in the suburbs of the city.
   その博覧会の開催場所は市の郊外に位置している。

2. The real estate company (　　　　　　　) for new office furniture.
   その不動産会社は新しいオフィス家具を注文した。

3. Nancy (　　　　　　　) for a two-day workshop on quality control.
   ナンシーは品質管理に関する2日間の講習会に参加登録した。

4. The staff of the public relations department (　　　　　　　) a press conference.
   広報部のスタッフが記者会見をセッティングした。

5. Jane (　　　　　　　) a questionnaire about the city's water, electricity, and gas rates.
   ジェインは市の水道・電気・ガス料金に関するアンケートに必要事項を記入した。

6. All attendees invited to the ceremony arrived (　　　　　　　).
   式典に招待された出席者全員が時間通りに到着した。

7. Mary (　　　　　　　) her suit at the dry cleaners on her way home.
   メアリは帰宅途中にクリーニング店にスーツを取りに行った。

8. Ray (　　　　　　　) the project with the staff from headquarters.
   レイは本社のスタッフとそのプロジェクトに取り組んだ。

9. Please (　　　　　　　) check that the refund has been credited to your account.
   返金がお客さまの口座に振り込まれていることを必ずご確認ください。

10. Susie was given a full description of her work responsibilities (　　　　　　　).
    スージーは前もって自分の職責の十分な説明を受けた。

---

☐ be located (in/on/etc)　☐ make sure that 節／be sure to 不定詞
☐ fill out　　　　　　　☐ on time　☐ place an order (for)　☐ sign up (for)
☐ in advance　　　　　　☐ pick up　☐ set up　　　　　　　☐ work on

## 15-C

音声を聴き、英文の空欄にあてはまる語句を入れ、その語句に該当する日本語を○で囲みましょう。
（語句中の単語は必要に応じて変化させましょう。）

🎧89

1. The town's botanical garden held an event that (　　　　　) children.
   町の植物園は子ども向けのイベントを開催した。

2. Cathy (　　　　　) mentor new employees working at the theater.
   キャシーは劇場で働く新人従業員を快く指導した。

3. Emily (　　　　　) running the employment agency.
   エミリーはその職業紹介所を運営する担当だ。

4. Jim (　　　　　) the new system on the assembly line.
   ジムは組み立てラインの新しいシステムにくわしい。

5. (　　　　　) a decline in sales, the board of directors held a special meeting.
   売上が落ちたせいで、取締役会は臨時の会議を開いた。

🎧90

6. Our grocery store no longer has that item (　　　　　).
   われわれの食料雑貨店にはその商品の在庫はもうありません。

7. (　　　　　) the waiting time at baggage claim, we could be late for the convention.
   手荷物受取所での待ち時間を考慮すると、われわれは会議に遅れるかもしれない。

8. Tom (　　　　　) the human resources department to drop off the memo from his boss.
   トムは上司からの社内連絡文書を届けるために人事部に立ち寄った。

9. The conference call (　　　　　) be held yesterday.
   その電話会議は昨日開催されることになっていた。

10. You can post a comment of (　　　　　) 50 words on this website.
    このウェブサイトには最大で50語までのコメントを投稿することができます。

---

☐ be familiar with　　☐ be supposed to 不定詞　　☐ given 名詞/that 節
☐ be in charge of　　☐ be willing to 不定詞　　☐ in stock
☐ be intended for　　☐ due to 名詞　　☐ stop by　　☐ up to 名詞

# 15-D

● この Unit で取り扱っている意味の熟語・構文の類義表現になるように、指定された出だしの文字で始まる1語を空所に書き込みましょう。ただし、空所の前に⇔の記号がある場合には反意表現になるようにしましょう。また、26) から 30) までは指示にしたがって解答しましょう。

1) pick up
　　　c_____
2) pick up ⇔ d_____ off
3) be located in
　　　be s_____ in
4) make sure that 節
　　　e_____ that 節
5) be sure to 不定詞
　　　m_____ sure to 不定詞
6) sign up for
　　　e_____ in
7) sign up for
　　　r_____ for
8) fill out
　　　c_____
9) fill out
　　　fill i_____
10) in advance
　　　b_____
11) on time
　　　p_____
12) on time
　　　p_____
13) on time ⇔ l_____
14) place an order for
　　　o_____
15) be intended for
　　　be d_____ for

16) in stock
　　　a_____
17) in stock ⇔ o_____ of stock
18) due to
　　　as a r_____ of
19) due to
　　　b_____ of
20) due to
　　　t_____ to
21) stop by
　　　c_____ by
22) stop by
　　　d_____ by
23) be familiar with
　　　be a_____ with
24) be in charge of
　　　be r_____ for
25) given 名詞/that 節
　　　c_____ 名詞/that 節
26) locate の名詞形
　　　_____
27) sign の名詞形
　　　_____
28) intend の名詞形
　　　_____
29) familiar の動詞形
　　　_____
30) advance の形容詞形
　　　_____

# TOEIC® Part 1 頻出の単語・熟語・定型表現 20

| | | |
|---|---|---|
| 1. | **drawer**<br>引き出し | The woman is opening a **drawer**.<br>女性が引き出しを開けようとしている。 |
| 2. | **ceiling**<br>天井 | Some plants have been hung from the **ceiling**.<br>植物がいくつか天井からつり下げられている。 |
| 3. | **stairs**<br>階段［階と階をつなぐ］ | A woman is walking down the **stairs**.<br>女性が階段を下りているところだ。 |
| 4. | **cashier**<br>レジ係 | The shopper is handing some money to the **cashier**.<br>買い物客がお金をレジ係に手渡している。 |
| 5. | **doorway**<br>出入り口 | The **doorway** to the room has been decorated.<br>部屋への出入り口には装飾が施されている。 |
| 6. | **ladder**<br>はしご | A **ladder** is lying on the ground.<br>はしごが地面に置かれている。 |
| 7. | **sign**<br>標識 | Workers are putting up a **sign** at an intersection.<br>作業員が交差点で標識を掲げようとしている。 |
| 8. | **steps**<br>階段［段数が少ない屋外の］ | One of the men is sitting on the porch **steps**.<br>男性のひとりが玄関ポーチの階段に座っている。 |
| 9. | **hang**<br>掛ける | They are **hanging** a painting on the wall.<br>彼らは壁に絵画を掛けようとしている。 |
| 10. | **stack**<br>積み重ねる［きれいに］ | Some boxes are **stacked** on the filing cabinet.<br>箱がいくつか書類整理棚の上に積み重ねられている。 |

| 11. **arrange**<br>きちんと並べる | The women are **arranging** shoes in a display window.<br>女性たちはショーウィンドウに靴をきちんと並べている。 |
| --- | --- |
| 12. **assemble**<br>組み立てる | The man is **assembling** some office chairs.<br>男性が事務用の椅子をいくつか組み立てている。 |
| 13. **pile**<br>積み重ねる [乱雑に] | Clothes are **piled** on top of each other.<br>衣服が積み重ねられている。 |
| 14. **fold**<br>折りたたむ | There are some **folded** clothes on the store shelves.<br>折りたたまれた衣類が店の棚にある。 |
| 15. **pour**<br>注ぐ | The server is **pouring** coffee into a cup.<br>給仕がコーヒーをカップに注いでいる。 |
| 16. **sweep**<br>掃く | One of the women is **sweeping** a patio.<br>女性のひとりがテラスを掃いている。 |
| 17. **lean against**<br>寄りかかる | She is **leaning against** the doorway to the kitchen.<br>彼女は台所の戸口に寄りかかっている。 |
| 18. **put away**<br>片付ける | A man is **putting away** a laptop in his backpack.<br>男性はリュックにノートパソコンを片付けようとしている。 |
| 19. **under construction**<br>建設中の | The bridge is currently **under construction**.<br>その橋は現在建設中だ。 |
| 20. **vending machine**<br>自動販売機 | **Vending machines** are lined up against the wall.<br>自動販売機が壁際に一列に並べられている。 |

# 第2部

## スコア 550 ➡ 650 をめざす 300 の語と表現

# UNIT 16
## 名詞 9

**16-A** それぞれの英単語の意味に最も当てはまる日本語を選びましょう。

1) opening [óʊpnɪŋ] _____
2) operation [ɑ̀:pəréɪʃən] _____
3) organization [ɔ̀:rɡənəzéɪʃən] _____
4) pharmacy [fɑ́:rməsi] _____
5) reference [réfərəns] _____
6) strategy [strǽtədʒi] _____
7) applicant [ǽplɪkənt] _____
8) architect [ɑ́:rkətèkt] _____
9) arrangement [əréɪndʒmənt] _____
10) fund [fʌ́nd] _____

11) instructions [ɪnstrʌ́kʃənz] _____
12) issue [íʃu:] _____
13) power [páʊər] _____
14) region [ríːdʒən] _____
15) requirement [rɪkwáɪərmənt] _____
16) vendor [véndər] _____
17) associate [əsóʊʃiət] _____
18) issue [íʃu:] _____
19) itinerary [aɪtínərèri] _____
20) mayor [méɪər] _____

| | | | |
|---|---|---|---|
| 空き [仕事の] | 応募者 | 供給業者 | 業務 |
| 建築家 | 号 | 資金 | 指示 |
| 市長 | 照会（先） | 戦略 | 団体 |
| 地域 | 手配 | 電力 | 同僚 |
| 必要条件 | 問題 | 薬局 | 旅行日程（表） |

## 16-B
音声を聴き、英文の空所にあてはまる単語を入れ、その単語に該当する日本語を〇で囲みましょう。
（単語は必要に応じて変化させましょう。）

🎧95

1. Given the decline in sales, we need a new marketing (　　　　　).
   売上の減少を考えれば、われわれには新しい市場戦略が必要だ。

2. Be sure to send a CV with a list of (　　　　　).
   履歴書は必ず照会先一覧といっしょに送ってください。

3. Kate is in charge of making travel (　　　　　).
   ケイトは出張の手配をする担当だ。

4. We've been working on reducing the cost of (　　　　　).
   当社は業務コストを削減することにずっと取り組んできた。

5. (　　　　　) must fill out an application form on our website.
   応募者は当社のウェブサイトの申込フォームに必要事項を記入しなければならない。

🎧96

6. There was a job (　　　　　) for an accountant.
   会計士の仕事の空きがあった。

7. James asked the (　　　　　) for an estimate for the office renovation.
   ジェイムズはその建築家にオフィスのリフォームの見積もりを依頼した。

8. The trade fair was hosted by a newly formed (　　　　　).
   その見本市は新しく結成された団体によって主催された。

9. According to the press release, the firm donated (　　　　　) to a charity.
   報道機関向け公式発表によると、その会社は慈善団体に資金を寄付した。

10. Our (　　　　　) has some of the cold medicine in stock.
    当薬局にはその風邪薬の在庫がいくらかございます。

---

| ☐ applicant | ☐ fund | ☐ organization | ☐ strategy |
| ☐ architect | ☐ opening | ☐ pharmacy | |
| ☐ arrangement | ☐ operation | ☐ reference | |

## 16-C

音声を聴き、英文の空所にあてはまる単語を入れ、その単語に該当する日本語を○で囲みましょう。
（単語は必要に応じて変化させましょう。）

1. Anne stopped by the store where her former ( ) worked.
   アンは元同僚が働いている店に立ち寄った。

2. A meeting was set up between the ( ) and residents.
   市長と住民のミーティングがセッティングされた。

3. Due to a lightning strike, the ( ) went out at the plant.
   落雷のせいで、その工場で電力が止まった。

4. The textile industry is thriving in the northern ( ) of the county.
   郡の北部地域では織物業が盛んだ。

5. I'm willing to find a different ( ).
   私が喜んで別の供給業者を見つけましょう。

6. Read the application ( ) for the job in advance.
   その職への申し込みの必要条件を前もって読んでください。

7. Fred placed an order for the next ( ) of the magazine.
   フレッドはその雑誌の次の号を注文した。

8. Mike is familiar with the ( ) the city has been addressing.
   マイクは市がずっと取り組んできた問題にくわしい。

9. She signed up for the convention following her supervisor's ( ).
   彼女は上司の指示にしたがって、その大会に参加登録した。

10. Lucy received a business trip ( ) with the clients' contact information.
    ルーシーは出張旅行日程表を顧客の連絡先とともに受け取った。

| ☐ associate | ☐ issue | ☐ power | ☐ vendor |
| ☐ instructions | ☐ itinerary | ☐ region | |
| ☐ issue | ☐ mayor | ☐ requirement | |

## 16-D

● それぞれの語の類義語を、このUNITの見出し語から選びましょう。

1) candidate _____
2) colleague _____
3) directions _____
4) edition _____
5) problem _____

● それぞれの語の動詞形を書きましょう。

1) arrangement _____
2) operation _____
3) organization _____
4) reference _____
5) requirement _____

## 16-E

空所に入る最も適切な語を選びましょう。ただし、それぞれの語の意味はこのUNITで取り扱ったものとします。

1. The company decided to develop its unique advertising ------.

    (A) applicant (B) architect (C) fund (D) strategy

2. There is a short-term ------ in the public relations department.

    (A) arrangement (B) mayor (C) opening (D) power

3. Bill contacted the local ------ to order more office supplies.

    (A) instructions (B) issue (C) requirement (D) vendor

4. Sally handed me a copy of the ------ and round-trip airplane tickets.

    (A) associate (B) itinerary (C) organization (D) pharmacy

5. There was heavy rain across the ------ last night.

    (A) issue (B) operation (C) reference (D) region

# UNIT 17
## 動詞 5

**17-A** それぞれの英単語の意味に最も当てはまる日本語を選びましょう。

1) **notify** [nóʊtəfàɪ] _____

2) **postpone** [poʊstpóʊn] _____

3) **edit** [édət] _____

4) **imply** [ɪmpláɪ] _____

5) **serve** [sə́ːrv] _____

6) **relocate** [rìːloʊkéɪt] _____

7) **apologize (for)** [əpɑ́ːlədʒàɪz] _____

8) **donate** [dóʊneɪt] _____

9) **inspect** [ɪnspékt] _____

10) **renew** [rɪn(j)úː] _____

11) **address** [ədrés] _____

12) **guarantee** [gèrəntíː] _____

13) **seek** [síːk] _____

14) **store** [stɔ́ːr] _____

15) **vote** [vóʊt] _____

16) **attach** [ətǽtʃ] _____

17) **handle** [hǽndl] _____

18) **load** [lóʊd] _____

19) **maintain** [meɪntéɪn] _____

20) **anticipate** [æntísəpèɪt] _____

---

| 暗に示す | 維持管理する | 移転する | 延期する |
| 寄付する | 検査する | 更新する | 探し求める |
| 謝罪する | 対処する [落ち着いて扱う] | 出す [食事を] | 通知する |
| 積む [荷物を] | 添付する | 投票する | 取り組む [難問に立ち向かう] |
| 保管する | 保証する | 編集する | 予期する |

## 17-B

音声を聴き、英文の空所にあてはまる単語を入れ、その単語に該当する日本語を○で囲みましょう。
（単語は必要に応じて変化させましょう。）

**101**

1. We ( donated ) some office equipment to a charity organization.
   当社は慈善団体にオフィス機器を寄付した。

2. Ellen ( edits ) a travel magazine for young people.
   エレンは若者向けの旅行雑誌を編集している。

3. The factory ( renewed ) the contract with the power company.
   その工場は電力会社と契約を更新した。

4. Meals were ( served ) on schedule during the flight.
   フライト中はスケジュール通りに食事が出された。

5. The company ( postponed ) outsourcing some of its operations.
   その会社は業務の一部を外注することを延期した。

**102**

6. David ( notified ) the applicants of the interview schedule.
   デイビッドは応募者に面接のスケジュールを通知した。

7. The mayor ordered the health department to ( inspect ) the facility.
   市長は保健部にその施設を検査するよう命じた。

8. The vendor ( apologized ) for the delay in delivery.
   その供給業者は納品の遅れのことで謝罪した。

9. What is ( implied ) about the instructions from the architect?
   建築家からの指示についてどのようなことが暗に示されていますか。

10. The pharmacy ( relocated ) to a neighboring town.
    その薬局は隣町に移転した。

---

☐ apologize (for)   ☐ imply      ☐ postpone   ☐ serve
☐ donate            ☐ inspect    ☐ relocate
☐ edit              ☐ notify     ☐ renew

## 17-C

音声を聴き、英文の空所にあてはまる単語を入れ、その単語に該当する日本語を○で囲みましょう。
（単語は必要に応じて変化させましょう。）

1. We are ( seeking ) an accountant who meets the following requirements.
   われわれは以下の必要条件を満たす会計士を探し求めています。

2. We've been ( addressing ) local environmental issues.
   当社は地元の環境問題に取り組んできました。

3. We ( maintain ) the roads in the mountain region of the city.
   われわれは市の山間地域の道路を維持管理している。

4. George ( stored ) old issues of the magazine on the shelf.
   ジョージはその雑誌の古い号を棚に保管した。

5. My associate ( handled ) inquiries from the client.
   私の同僚がその顧客からの問い合わせに対処した。

6. Can I see the list of references the applicant ( attached )?
   その応募者が添付した照会先リストを見せてもらえますか。

7. Our electronics store ( guarantees ) the lowest prices.
   当家電店は最低価格を保証します。

8. John ( loaded ) the cardboard boxes containing beverages into the van.
   ジョンは飲料が入った段ボール箱をワゴン車に積んだ。

9. The board ( voted ) on a new advertising strategy.
   役員会は新しい広告戦略に関して投票した。

10. The event raised more funds than we had ( anticipated ).
    そのイベントはわれわれが予期していたよりも多くの資金を集めた。

---

| ☐ address | ☐ guarantee | ☐ maintain | ☐ vote |
| ☐ anticipate | ☐ handle | ☐ seek | |
| ☐ attach | ☐ load | ☐ store | |

## 17-D

- それぞれの語の類義語を、このUNITの見出し語から選びましょう。

1) contribute _____
2) delay _____
3) examine _____
4) inform _____
5) suggest _____

- それぞれの語の名詞形を書きましょう。

1) attach _____
2) edit _____
3) relocate _____
4) renew _____
5) serve _____

## 17-E

空所に入る最も適切な語を選びましょう。ただし、それぞれの語の意味はこのUNITで取り扱ったものとします。

1. Would you ------ these packages into the back seat of the car?

   (A) apologize for   (B) imply   (C) load   (D) maintain

2. The residents urged the mayor to ------ the traffic noise problem.

   (A) address   (B) attach   (C) donate   (D) guarantee

3. Laura helped Mary to ------ the extra office supplies in the cabinet.

   (A) anticipate   (B) notify   (C) store   (D) vote

4. We ------ an experienced graphic designer for our new business.

   (A) edit   (B) inspect   (C) postpone   (D) seek

5. The supervisor asked Nancy to ------ the customers' complaints about the service.

   (A) handle   (B) relocate   (C) renew   (D) serve

# UNIT 18
## 名詞 10

**18-A** それぞれの英単語の意味に最も当てはまる日本語を選びましょう。

1) **newsletter** [n(j)ú:zlètər]

2) **payroll** [péɪròʊl]

3) **professor** [prəfésər]

4) **supplier** [səpláɪər]

5) **admission** [ədmíʃən]

6) **developer** [dɪvéləpər]

7) **employment** [ɪmplɔ́ɪmənt]

8) **fabric** [fǽbrɪk]

9) **inspector** [ɪnspéktər]

10) **permission** [pərmíʃən]

11) **permit** [pə́:rmɪt]

12) **recommendation** [rèkəməndéɪʃən]

13) **subscription** [səbskrípʃən]

14) **aisle** [áɪl]

15) **committee** [kəmíti]

16) **consumer** [kəns(j)ú:mər]

17) **exhibit** [ɪgzíbɪt]

18) **flyer** [fláɪər]

19) **publication** [pʌ̀bləkéɪʃən]

20) **reception** [rɪsépʃən]

| | | | |
|---|---|---|---|
| 委員会 | 開発者 | 会報 | 歓迎会 |
| 給与（支払名簿） | 供給業者 | 教授 | 許可 |
| 許可証 | 検査官 | 雇用 | 出版（物） |
| 消費者 | 推薦（状） | チラシ | 通路 |
| 定期購読 | 展示会 | 入場（料） | 布地 |

## 18-B 音声を聴き、英文の空所にあてはまる単語を入れ、その単語に該当する日本語を○で囲みましょう。
（単語は必要に応じて変化させましょう。）

1. The business plans to hire up to five new software ( developers ).
   その企業は5名まで新しいソフトウェア開発者を雇う計画をしている。

2. This durable ( fabric ) is guaranteed to last for decades.
   この耐久性のある布地は数十年間長持ちすることを保証します。

3. The company's total monthly ( payroll ) exceeds $100 million.
   その会社の毎月の給与の総額は1億ドルを超える。

4. The ( supplier ) handled an urgent order from the manufacturer.
   その供給業者はメーカーからの急な注文に対処した。

5. The sales manager obtained ( permission ) to fill the vacancy.
   営業部長は欠員を補充する許可を得た。

6. Ray is currently seeking full-time ( employment ).
   レイは現在正社員での雇用を求めている。

7. Mary is busy editing the company's ( newsletter ).
   メアリは会社の会報を編集するのにいそがしい。

8. ( Admission ) to the museum is included in the tour price.
   その美術館への入場料はツアー代に含まれている。

9. The safety ( inspectors ) notified the factory of their planned visit.
   保安検査官たちはその工場に彼らの訪問予定を通知した。

10. The company donated funds to the ( professor ) for his lab.
    その会社はその教授の研究室に資金を寄付した。

---

☐ admission     ☐ fabric      ☐ payroll      ☐ supplier
☐ developer     ☐ inspector   ☐ permission
☐ employment    ☐ newsletter  ☐ professor

## 18-C

音声を聴き、英文の空所にあてはまる単語を入れ、その単語に該当する日本語を○で囲みましょう。
（単語は必要に応じて変化させましょう。）

1. The city's education ( ) voted on a new educational policy.
   市の教育委員会は新しい教育政策に関して投票をした。

2. The time to renew your newspaper ( ) is coming up.
   お客さまの新聞の定期購読を更新する時期が近づいて参りました。

3. A delicious meal was served at the ( ).
   歓迎会でおいしい食事が提供された。

4. The gallery ( ) had more visitors than anticipated.
   画廊での展示会には予想していたよりも多くの人が訪れた。

5. I saw a ( ) saying the restaurant was relocating.
   私はそのレストランが移転するというチラシを見た。

6. Be sure to attach a letter of ( ).
   必ず推薦状を添付してください。

7. The ( ) of Susie's first book was postponed.
   スージーの最初の本の出版は延期された。

8. The shopping cart was left in the middle of the ( ).
   ショッピングカートが通路の真ん中に放置されていた。

9. Nancy picked up a parking ( ) at reception.
   ナンシーは受付に駐車許可証を取りに行った。

10. The manufacturer apologized to ( ) for the product defect.
    そのメーカーは消費者に製品の欠陥のことで謝罪した。

---

| ☐ aisle | ☐ exhibit | ☐ publication | ☐ subscription |
| ☐ committee | ☐ flyer | ☐ reception | |
| ☐ consumer | ☐ permit | ☐ recommendation | |

## 18-D

● それぞれの語の類義語を、このUNITの見出し語から選びましょう。

1) cloth _____
2) commission _____
3) entrance _____
4) license _____
5) vendor _____

● それぞれの語の動詞形を書きましょう。

1) consumer _____
2) employment _____
3) publication _____
4) reception _____
5) subscription _____

## 18-E

空所に入る最も適切な語を選びましょう。ただし、それぞれの語の意味はこのUNITで取り扱ったものとします。

1. Please make sure to subscribe to our store's free online ------.

   (A) committee         (B) fabric
   (C) newsletter        (D) recommendation

2. Tom wrote down the phone number on the edge of the ------.

   (A) admission    (B) employment    (C) flyer    (D) professor

3. When will the building ------ come to check our factory?

   (A) consumer    (B) inspector    (C) payroll    (D) subscription

4. Cathy requested ------ to leave early from her supervisor.

   (A) developer    (B) exhibit    (C) permission    (D) reception

5. The medicine is on the middle shelf at the end of this ------.

   (A) aisle    (B) permit    (C) publication    (D) supplier

# UNIT 19
## 形容詞 2

### 19-A それぞれの英単語の意味に最も当てはまる日本語を選びましょう。

1) **multiple** [mʌ́ltəpl]
2) **technical** [téknɪkl]
3) **experienced** [ɪkspíəriənst]
4) **inexpensive** [ìnɪkspénsɪv]
5) **advanced** [ədvǽnst]
6) **express** [ɪksprés]
7) **mobile** [móʊbl]
8) **on-site** [ɑ́:nsàɪt]
9) **temporary** [témpərèri]
10) **innovative** [ínəvèɪtɪv]

11) **outstanding** [àʊtstǽndɪŋ]
12) **qualified** [kwɑ́:ləfàɪd]
13) **valid** [vǽlɪd]
14) **related** [rɪléɪtɪd]
15) **affordable** [əfɔ́:rdəbl]
16) **commercial** [kəmə́:rʃəl]
17) **industrial** [ɪndʌ́striəl]
18) **legal** [lí:gl]
19) **regional** [rí:dʒənl]
20) **extensive** [ɪksténsɪv]

---

| | | | |
|---|---|---|---|
| 一時的な | 買える値段の | 革新的な | 関連した |
| 技術の | 際立った | 経験豊富な | 携帯電話の |
| 現場の | 工業（用）の | 資格がある | 商業（用）の |
| 進んだ | 速達の | 地域の | 幅広い |
| 複数の | 法律の | 安い [品質の割に] | 有効な |

## 19-B
音声を聴き、英文の空所にあてはまる単語を入れ、その単語に該当する日本語を○で囲みましょう。
（単語は必要に応じて変化させましょう。）

🎧 113

1. The posters and flyers were sent by ( ) courier.
   そのポスターとチラシは速達の宅配便で送られた。

2. The hotel offers surprisingly ( ) meals and accommodation.
   そのホテルは驚くほど安い食事と宿泊を提供している。

3. The ( ) manager attended an investigation conducted by the inspector.
   現場のマネジャーが検査官による調査に立ち会った。

4. The professor provided ( ) support for the company.
   教授はその会社に技術支援を提供した。

5. Several ( ) artists participated in the museum exhibit.
   多くの革新的な芸術家がその美術館での展示会に参加した。

🎧 114

6. What is implied about the ( ) features of the laptop?
   そのノートパソコンの進んだ特徴についてどのようなことが示唆されていますか。

7. An ( ) plumber inspected the bathroom in Kate's house.
   経験豊富な配管工がケイトの家のバスルームを検査した。

8. Laura found ( ) employment at a supermarket.
   ローラはスーパーでの一時的な職を得た。

9. The software developer is familiar with ( ) programming languages.
   そのソフトウェア開発者は複数のプログラミング言語をよく知っている。

10. Jack downloaded the ( ) app to use the company's subscription service.
    ジャックはその会社のサブスクサービスを利用するためにその携帯電話アプリをダウンロードした。

---

| ☐ advanced | ☐ inexpensive | ☐ multiple | ☐ temporary |
| ☐ experienced | ☐ innovative | ☐ on-site | |
| ☐ express | ☐ mobile | ☐ technical | |

## 19-C

音声を聴き、英文の空所にあてはまる単語を入れ、その単語に該当する日本語を○で囲みましょう。
（単語は必要に応じて変化させましょう。）

1. The ( commercial ) property rented by the supplier is being renovated.
   その供給業者が賃借しているその商業用物件はリフォーム中だ。

2. Bill considered publishing a new magazine featuring ( regional ) cuisine.
   ビルは地域の料理を特集する新雑誌を出版することを検討した。

3. The discount admission coupon is ( valid ) for one month.
   その入場割引券は1か月間有効だ。

4. This ( extensive ) product promotion will attract consumer attention.
   この幅広い製品販促活動は消費者の注目を集めるだろう。

5. Sally addressed issues facing the company in its ( legal ) department.
   サリーは法務部で会社が直面している問題に取り組んだ。

6. Fred stored the applicants' résumés and ( related ) documents in the cabinet.
   フレッドは応募者の履歴書と関連書類を整理棚に保管した。

7. James' ( outstanding ) contribution was mentioned in the company newsletter.
   ジェイムズの際立った貢献が社内報に書かれた。

8. Lucy has been looking for an ( affordable ) house in the district.
   ルーシーはその地区で買える値段の家をずっと探している。

9. Mike requested permission to use the ( industrial ) design in the project.
   マイクはプロジェクトでその工業デザインを使うための許可を求めた。

10. Anne is ( qualified ) for selection as a committee member.
    アンは委員会のメンバーに選ばれる資格がある。

☐ affordable ☐ industrial ☐ qualified ☐ valid
☐ commercial ☐ legal ☐ regional
☐ extensive ☐ outstanding ☐ related

## 19-D

● それぞれの語の類義語を、このUNITの見出し語から選びましょう。

1) excellent _____
2) local _____
3) relevant _____
4) several _____
5) short-term _____

● それぞれの語の名詞形を書きましょう。

1) industrial _____
2) innovative _____
3) qualified _____
4) related _____
5) technical _____

## 19-E

空所に入る最も適切な語を選びましょう。ただし、それぞれの語の意味はこのUNITで取り扱ったものとします。

1. Applicants must have more than five years of experience and a ------ teaching license.

    (A) commercial    (B) mobile    (C) multiple    (D) valid

2. David resigned to pursue an ------ degree at the university.

    (A) advanced    (B) affordable    (C) extensive    (D) on-site

3. Our online store can deliver goods via ------ mail for an additional charge.

    (A) express    (B) innovative    (C) outstanding    (D) technical

4. Please log in with this ------ password within 30 minutes.

    (A) industrial    (B) qualified    (C) regional    (D) temporary

5. Our music school is currently seeking ------ piano instructors.

    (A) experienced    (B) inexpensive    (C) legal    (D) related

# UNIT 20
## 名詞 11

**20-A** それぞれの英単語の意味に最も当てはまる日本語を選びましょう。

🎧 117
1) **refreshments** [rɪfréʃmənts] _____
2) **solution** [səlúːʃən] _____
3) **accountant** [əkáʊntnt] _____
4) **complex** [káːmpleks] _____
5) **directions** [dərékʃənz] _____
6) **investment** [ɪnvéstmənt] _____
7) **official** [əfíʃəl] _____
8) **subscriber** [səbskráɪbər] _____
9) **broadcast** [brɔ́ːdkæst] _____
10) **container** [kəntéɪnər] _____

🎧 118
11) **intern** [íntəːrn] _____
12) **performance** [pərfɔ́ːrməns] _____
13) **quantity** [kwáːntəti] _____
14) **refrigerator [fridge]** [rɪfrídʒərèɪtər] _____
15) **regulation** [règjəléɪʃən] _____
16) **achievement** [ətʃíːvmənt] _____
17) **association** [əsòʊsiéɪʃən] _____
18) **certificate** [sərtífɪkət] _____
19) **degree** [dɪgríː] _____
20) **demand** [dɪmǽnd] _____

| | | | |
|---|---|---|---|
| 会計士 | 解決策 | 学位 | 軽い飲食物 |
| 規則 | 協会 | 業績［実力による成績］ | 業績［努力で成し遂げた偉業］ |
| 実習生 | 需要 | 証明書 | 定期購読者 |
| 投資 | 複合施設 | 放送（番組） | 道順 |
| 役人 | 容器 | 量 | 冷蔵庫 |

## 20-B
音声を聴き、英文の空所にあてはまる単語を入れ、その単語に該当する日本語を○で囲みましょう。
（単語は必要に応じて変化させましょう。）

1. The government (            ) checked the company's payroll.
   政府の役人たちがその会社の給与支払名簿を調べた。

2. This mobile app will provide the best (          ) to your destination.
   この携帯電話アプリは目的地までの最善の道順を提供します。

3. (          ) were served at the reception for new employees.
   新入社員の歓迎会では軽い飲食物が出された。

4. The experienced technical team was responsible for the live TV (          ).
   経験豊富な技術チームがその生放送のテレビ番組を担当した。

5. The company obtained a construction permit for the sports (          ).
   その会社はスポーツ複合施設の建設許可証を得た。

6. Ellen proposed an innovative (          ) to the legal issue.
   エレンはその法的な問題への革新的な解決策を提案した。

7. The caterer loaded some food (          ) into the van.
   そのケータリング業者は料理の入った容器をライトバンに積んだ。

8. The firm made an (          ) in some commercial properties.
   その会社はいくつかの商業用物件に投資した。

9. George has extensive experience as an (          ).
   ジョージには会計士としての幅広い経験がある。

10. The number of (          ) to our newspaper has been decreasing.
    われわれの新聞の定期購読者の数は減ってきている。

---

☐ accountant    ☐ container    ☐ official    ☐ subscriber
☐ broadcast    ☐ directions    ☐ refreshments
☐ complex    ☐ investment    ☐ solution

## 20-C

音声を聴き、英文の空所にあてはまる単語を入れ、その単語に該当する日本語を○で囲みましょう。
（単語は必要に応じて変化させましょう。）

🎧 121

1. Please send a copy of a valid ( ) by express mail.
   有効な証明書の写し一通を速達で送ってください。

2. The firm joined a regional ( ) of manufacturers.
   その会社はメーカーで作る地域の協会に加わった。

3. The increasing ( ) for coal is considered to be temporary.
   石炭の需要の増加は一時的なものと見なされている。

4. The plant uses a large ( ) of industrial chemicals.
   その工場は多量の工業用化学薬品を使用する。

5. We are in compliance with national safety ( ).
   当社は国の安全規則を遵守しております。

🎧 122

6. Applicants must have an advanced ( ) in a related field.
   応募者は関連分野での上級学位が必要です。

7. Huge sales of the new product improved the company's ( ).
   新商品のばく大な売上は会社の業績を改善させた。

8. The new ( ) are receiving on-site training.
   新しい実習生たちは実地訓練を受けているところだ。

9. This state-of-the-art ( ) is affordable.
   この最新の冷蔵庫は買える値段だ。

10. Linda was recognized for her outstanding ( ) at the sales competition.
    リンダは販売コンテストでの際立った業績で表彰された。

| ☐ achievement | ☐ degree | ☐ performance | ☐ regulation |
| ☐ association | ☐ demand | ☐ quantity | |
| ☐ certificate | ☐ intern | ☐ refrigerator | |

## 20-D

- それぞれの語の類義語を、このUNITの見出し語から選びましょう。

1) amount _____
2) answer _____
3) holder _____
4) organization _____
5) rule _____

- それぞれの語の動詞形を書きましょう。

1) achievement _____
2) directions _____
3) investment _____
4) performance _____
5) subscriber _____

## 20-E

空所に入る最も適切な語を選びましょう。ただし、それぞれの語の意味はこのUNITで取り扱ったものとします。

1. The conference organizers served complimentary ------ at the social gathering.

    (A) broadcast        (B) directions        (C) performance        (D) refreshments

2. A cinema ------ is being built within walking distance of the station.

    (A) achievement      (B) complex          (C) container          (D) investment

3. Mary struggled to complete her university ------ in hospitality management.

    (A) accountant       (B) degree           (C) official           (D) quantity

4. In which department has the new ------ been working for the past few weeks?

    (A) association      (B) certificate      (C) intern             (D) subscriber

5. The company is doing well because of the increase in ------ for solar power generators.

    (A) demand           (B) refrigerator     (C) regulation         (D) solution

# UNIT 21
## 動詞 6

**21-A** それぞれの英単語の意味に最も当てはまる日本語を選びましょう。

1) **apply (to)** [əpláɪ]

2) **enroll (in)** [ɪnróʊl]

3) **expect** [ɪkspékt]

4) **run** [rʌ́n]

5) **track** [trǽk]

6) **verify** [vérəfàɪ]

7) **appreciate** [əpríːʃièɪt]

8) **establish** [ɪstǽblɪʃ]

9) **estimate** [éstəmèɪt]

10) **invest (in)** [ɪnvést]

11) **involve** [ɪnvɑ́ːlv]

12) **launch** [lɔ́ːntʃ]

13) **manufacture** [mæ̀njəfǽktʃər]

14) **undergo** [ʌ̀ndərgóʊ]

15) **implement** [ímpləmènt]

16) **issue** [íʃuː]

17) **accommodate** [əkɑ́ːmədèɪt]

18) **highlight** [háɪlàɪt]

19) **accommodate** [əkɑ́ːmədèɪt]

20) **carry** [kéri]

---

| | | | |
|---|---|---|---|
| ありがたく思う | 受ける | 運営する | 開始する |
| 期待する | 強調する | 実行する | 収容する |
| 製造する | 設立する | 対応する | 確かめる |
| 追跡する | 適用される | 投資する | 登録する |
| 伴う | 取り扱う [商品を] | 発行する | 見積もる |

## 21-B
音声を聴き、英文の空所にあてはまる単語を入れ、その単語に該当する日本語を○で囲みましょう。
（単語は必要に応じて変化させましょう。）

1. John ( ) in an online investment seminar.
   ジョンはオンライン投資セミナーに登録した。

2. Jane ( ) in a company that manages several shopping complexes.
   ジェインは多くのショッピング複合施設を運営する会社に投資した。

3. I would ( ) it if you would reply as soon as possible.
   できるだけ早くお返事いただければありがたく思います。

4. The intern is ( ) to be recruited as a full-time employee.
   その実習生は正社員として採用されることを期待している。

5. The street maintenance cost more than city officials had ( ).
   その街路の保守整備には市の役人たちが見積もっていたよりも費用がかかった。

6. Susie ( ) that the candidate was qualified for the promotion.
   スージーはその候補者が昇進する資格があることを確かめた。

7. A 10% discount ( ) to people who subscribe for longer than a year.
   10%の割引は定期購読を1年以上している方に適用されます。

8. There is an increased demand for software that can ( ) orders.
   注文品を追跡できるソフトウェアの需要が増えている。

9. Nancy ( ) a coffee shop that offers light meals.
   ナンシーは軽食を提供するカフェを運営している。

10. The broadcast studio was ( ) decades ago.
    その放送スタジオは数十年前に設立された。

| ☐ apply (to) | ☐ establish | ☐ invest (in) | ☐ verify |
| ☐ appreciate | ☐ estimate | ☐ run | |
| ☐ enroll (in) | ☐ expect | ☐ track | |

## 21-C

音声を聴き、英文の空所にあてはまる単語を入れ、その単語に該当する日本語を○で囲みましょう。
（単語は必要に応じて変化させましょう。）

🎧127

1. Our online bookstore (　　　　　　) a wide selection of publications.
   当オンライン書店は幅広い品揃えの出版物を取り扱っております。

2. Degree certificates may take up to one week to be (　　　　　　).
   学位証明書は発行されるのに最長で1週間かかる場合があります。

3. Some of the new employees need to (　　　　　　) additional training.
   新入社員の何名かは追加の研修を受ける必要がある。

4. This assistant accountant position (　　　　　　) a lot of traveling.
   この会計士補の職は多くの出張を伴います。

5. You should (　　　　　　) your team's achievements in the presentation.
   プレゼンではあなたのチームの功績を強調するべきだ。

🎧128

6. The plant (　　　　　　) a large quantity of plastic containers.
   その工場は多量のプラスティック製容器を製造している。

7. The hotel's main banquet hall can (　　　　　　) 500 people.
   そのホテルの大宴会場は500人を収容できる。

8. It'll take time to (　　　　　　) the solution to the problem.
   その問題の解決策を実行するには時間がかかるだろう。

9. The ad campaign for the new fridge is being (　　　　　　) this week.
   その新しい冷蔵庫の広告キャンペーンが今週開始されている。

10. The city tried to (　　　　　　) the increase in the number of foreign tourists.
    その市は外国からの観光客の増加に対応しようとした。

---

| ☐ accommodate | ☐ highlight | ☐ issue | ☐ undergo |
| ☐ accommodate | ☐ implement | ☐ launch | |
| ☐ carry | ☐ involve | ☐ manufacture | |

UNIT 21／動詞6

## 21-D

● それぞれの語の類義語を、この UNIT の見出し語から選びましょう。

1) experience _____
2) manage _____
3) produce _____
4) register _____
5) start _____

● それぞれの語の名詞形を書きましょう。

1) accommodate _____
2) apply _____
3) appreciate _____
4) establish _____
5) expect _____

## 21-E

空所に入る最も適切な語を選びましょう。ただし、それぞれの語の意味はこの UNIT で取り扱ったものとします。

1. Our supermarket chain will ------ organic produce from around the region.

　(A) appreciate　　(B) carry　　(C) implement　　(D) undergo

2. Cathy decided to ------ stocks of the courier company.

　(A) apply to　　(B) establish　　(C) invest in　　(D) manufacture

3. Tom's new position in the department will ------ training interns.

　(A) enroll in　　(B) involve　　(C) issue　　(D) track

4. We ------ that the city will have a population of about 300,000 by next year.

　(A) accommodate　　(B) estimate　　(C) highlight　　(D) run

5. Emily tried to ------ whether the information on the product's label was accurate.

　(A) accommodate　　(B) expect　　(C) launch　　(D) verify

# UNIT 22
## 名詞 12

**22-A** それぞれの英単語の意味に最も当てはまる日本語を選びましょう。

1) **deposit** [dɪpá:zət]

2) **instrument** [ínstrəmənt]

3) **insurance** [ɪnʃúərəns]

4) **promotion** [prəmóʊʃən]

5) **resources** [rí:sò:rsɪz]

6) **revenue** [révən(j)ù:]

7) **role** [róʊl]

8) **server** [sə́:rvər]

9) **source** [só:rs]

10) **status** [stǽtəs]

11) **summary** [sʌ́məri]

12) **analysis** [ənǽləsɪs]

13) **approval** [əprú:vl]

14) **division** [dɪvíʒən]

15) **draft** [drǽft]

16) **electricity** [ɪlèktrísəti]

17) **launch** [lɔ́:ntʃ]

18) **selection** [səlékʃən]

19) **tip** [típ]

20) **accomplishment** [əkɑ́:mplɪʃmənt]

| 概要 | 楽器 | 給仕係 | 業績 |
| 資源 | 下書き | 品揃え | 収益 |
| 状況 | 承認 | 手付金 | 出どころ |
| 電気 | 発売 | 販売促進 | 秘訣 |
| 部門 | 分析 | 保険 | 役割 |

UNIT 22／名詞 12　91

## 22-B

音声を聴き、英文の空所にあてはまる単語を入れ、その単語に該当する日本語を○で囲みましょう。
（単語は必要に応じて変化させましょう。）

1. The delivery ( status ) of your order can be tracked through our website.
   お客さまのご注文品の配達状況は当社のウェブサイトから追跡ができます。

2. We didn't have the necessary ( resources ) to complete the job on schedule.
   その仕事を予定どおりに完了させるための必要な資源がわれわれにはなかった。

3. I appreciate your sharing the ( source ) of the information.
   あなたがその情報の出どころを話してくださったことをありがたく思っております。

4. James launched a business that sells auto ( insurance ).
   ジェイムズは自動車保険を販売する事業を開始した。

5. Laura played a key ( role ) in implementing the marketing strategy.
   ローラはその市場戦略を実行する上で重要な役割を果たした。

6. Jim checked whether the musical ( instrument ) was valuable or not.
   ジムはその楽器が価値があるかどうかを確かめた。

7. The ( server ) at the café gave me directions to the museum.
   カフェの給仕係が私に美術館までの道順を教えてくれた。

8. Would you secure the item for me if I pay a ( deposit )?
   手付金を払えば、その商品を確保してもらえますか。

9. Kate expects the sales ( promotion ) to be successful.
   ケイトはその販売促進が成功することを期待している。

10. The firm's monthly ( revenue ) is estimated at $1 million.
    その会社の毎月の収益は 100 万ドルと見積もられている。

| ☐ deposit | ☐ promotion | ☐ role | ☐ status |
| ☐ instrument | ☐ resources | ☐ server | |
| ☐ insurance | ☐ revenue | ☐ source | |

## 22-C

音声を聴き、英文の空所にあてはまる単語を入れ、その単語に該当する日本語を○で囲みましょう。
（単語は必要に応じて変化させましょう。）

1. Manufacturing these garments requires a lot of water and ( electricity ).
   これらの衣類を製造するには多くの水と電気が必要だ。

2. Matt is proud of the ( accomplishments ) he has made over his career.
   マットは自分のキャリアにわたって成し遂げてきた業績を誇らしく思っている。

3. Here's a financial ( summary ) of the association that Linda runs.
   これがリンダが運営している協会の財政に関する概要だ。

4. Bill shared ( tips ) on getting more people to enroll in the course.
   ビルは講座により多くの人に登録してもらう秘訣を話した。

5. Anne requested ( approval ) for her business trip.
   アンは出張の承認を求めた。

6. Diners seem satisfied with the restaurant's dessert ( selection ).
   食事客はそのレストランのデザートの品揃えに満足しているようだ。

7. Mike finished a ( draft ) of the report for the company.
   マイクは会社への報告書の下書きを終えた。

8. Establishing the new ( division ) will involve a lot of staff transfers.
   その新部門を設立することには多くのスタッフの異動を伴うだろう。

9. Fred conducted an ( analysis ) of the properties he might invest in.
   フレッドは自分が投資するかもしれない不動産の分析をした。

10. As the editor, Sally felt very excited about the book ( launch ).
    編集者としてサリーはその本の発売にとてもわくわくした気持ちになった。

---

☐ accomplishment　☐ division　☐ launch　☐ tip
☐ analysis　☐ draft　☐ selection
☐ approval　☐ electricity　☐ summary

## 22-D

● それぞれの語の類義語を、このUNITの見出し語から選びましょう。

1) achievement _____
2) department _____
3) hint _____
4) income _____
5) overview _____
6) part _____
7) permission _____
8) power _____
9) range _____
10) situation _____

## 22-E

空所に入る最も適切な語を選びましょう。ただし、それぞれの語の意味はこのUNITで取り扱ったものとします。

1. Before you move in, you need three months' rent and six months' security ------.

    (A) deposit　　(B) launch　　(C) role　　(D) status

2. Following his friend's recommendation, David purchased life ------.

    (A) accomplishment　　　　(B) insurance
    (C) source　　　　　　　　(D) summary

3. You won't receive any emails regarding our store's latest ------ unless you register.

    (A) instrument　　(B) promotion　　(C) resources　　(D) server

4. I've just finished the final ------ of the contract.

    (A) draft　　(B) electricity　　(C) revenue　　(D) selection

5. Ellen conducted data ------ of the survey results with her colleague.

    (A) analysis　　(B) approval　　(C) division　　(D) tip

# UNIT 23
## 形容詞 3

### 23-A それぞれの英単語の意味に最も当てはまる日本語を選びましょう。

1) **fund-raising/fundraising** [fʌ́ndrèɪzɪŋ]
2) **ideal** [aɪdíːəl]
3) **quality** [kwάːləti]
4) **senior** [síːnjər]
5) **suitable** [súːtəbl]
6) **attractive** [ətrǽktɪv]
7) **competitive** [kəmpétətɪv]
8) **dental** [déntl]
9) **durable** [d(j)úərəbl]
10) **impressed** [ɪmprést]
11) **prospective** [prəspéktɪv]
12) **eager** [íːgər]
13) **extended** [ɪksténdɪd]
14) **initial** [ɪníʃəl]
15) **positive** [pάːzətɪv]
16) **reduced** [rɪd(j)úːst]
17) **secure** [sɪkjúər]
18) **administrative** [ədmínəstrèɪtɪv]
19) **challenging** [tʃǽlɪndʒɪŋ]
20) **confident** [kάːnfədənt]

| | | | |
|---|---|---|---|
| 安全な | 感銘を受けた | 管理の | 期間を延長した |
| 好意的な | 最初の | 歯科の | 資金集めの |
| 自信がある | 上位の | 耐久性のある | 大変だがやりがいのある |
| 他に負けない | 適切な | 熱心な | 見込みのある |
| 魅力的な | 理想的な | 良質の | 割引の |

## 23-B
音声を聴き、英文の空所にあてはまる単語を入れ、その単語に該当する日本語を○で囲みましょう。
（単語は必要に応じて変化させましょう。）

1. Our supermarket provides a wide selection of ( quality ) food.
   わたくしどものスーパーマーケットは良質の食品を幅広い品揃えで提供しております。

2. Nancy was ( impressed ) with the children's musical performance.
   ナンシーは子どもたちの音楽パフォーマンスに感銘を受けた。

3. We need to find a ( suitable ) replacement for our previous server.
   われわれは前の給仕係の適切な代わりの人を見つける必要がある。

4. George finished a draft of his speech for the ( fund-raising ) event.
   ジョージは資金集めのイベントで行うスピーチの下書きを終えた。

5. The financial status of the ( dental ) clinic is improving.
   その歯科医院の財政状況は良くなってきている。

6. Mary was promoted to a ( senior ) role in the division.
   メアリはその部門で上位の役職に昇進した。

7. The ( durable ) fabric became very popular and boosted the company's revenues.
   その耐久性のある布地が大変人気になり、その会社の収益を押し上げた。

8. The electricity company offers ( competitive ) salaries and benefits.
   その電力会社は他に負けない給与と手当を提供している。

9. The ( ideal ) venue for the performance is a big stadium.
   そのコンサートの理想的な開催場所は大きなスタジアムです。

10. The price of the company's auto insurance is ( attractive ).
    その会社の自動車保険の価格は魅力的だ。

---

☐ attractive  ☐ durable  ☐ impressed  ☐ senior
☐ competitive  ☐ fund-raising / fundraising  ☐ suitable
☐ dental  ☐ ideal  ☐ quality

## 23-C

音声を聴き、英文の空所にあてはまる単語を入れ、その単語に該当する日本語を○で囲みましょう。
（単語は必要に応じて変化させましょう。）

1. Identifying the source of the information is a ( challenging ) task.
   情報の出どころを特定することは大変だがやりがいのある任務だ。

2. Tom was ( confident ) that the project would get approval.
   トムはそのプロジェクトが承認を得ることに自信があった。

3. Jane was ( eager ) to collect data to help with the market analysis.
   ジェインは市場分析の助けになるデータを集めることに熱心だった。

4. We need to attract ( prospective ) customers with more in-store promotions.
   われわれは店舗でのより多くの販売促進活動で見込み客を引き付ける必要がある。

5. The management's response to the project summary was ( positive ).
   そのプロジェクトの概要への経営陣の反応は好意的だった。

6. Susie purchased the ( extended ) warranty for her new washing machine.
   スージーは新しい洗濯機の期間延長保証を購入した。

7. The consultant presented a ( secure ) way to manage company data.
   そのコンサルタントは会社のデータを管理する安全な方法を提示した。

8. Cathy was highly qualified for the ( administrative ) position.
   キャシーはその管理職に大変適任だった。

9. Here are some tips for making your ( initial ) investment in stocks.
   これが最初の株式投資をする際の秘訣です。

10. We offered a ( reduced ) price when we launched the new product.
    われわれがその新製品を発売したときは割引価格を提供した。

---

| ☐ administrative | ☐ eager | ☐ positive | ☐ secure |
| ☐ challenging | ☐ extended | ☐ prospective | |
| ☐ confident | ☐ initial | ☐ reduced | |

## 23-D

- それぞれの語の類義語を、このUNITの見出し語から選びましょう。

1) first _____
2) keen _____
3) long _____
4) perfect _____
5) potential _____

- それぞれの語の名詞形を書きましょう。

1) attractive _____
2) competitive _____
3) confident _____
4) durable _____
5) secure _____

## 23-E

空所に入る最も適切な語を選びましょう。ただし、それぞれの語の意味はこのUNITで取り扱ったものとします。

1. I'm calling to cancel my ------ appointment with your clinic.

   (A) attractive　　(B) dental　　(C) ideal　　(D) quality

2. Kate is one of the ------ analysts at the research institute.

   (A) durable　　(B) extended　　(C) impressed　　(D) senior

3. Mary respected her supervisor for having considerable ------ skills.

   (A) administrative　　(B) challenging　　(C) eager　　(D) initial

4. All of the reviews for the play in the next day's newspapers were ------.

   (A) competitive　　(B) fund-raising　　(C) positive　　(D) reduced

5. Our new jackets are washable and ------ for various occasions.

   (A) confident　　(B) prospective　　(C) secure　　(D) suitable

# UNIT 24
## 名詞 13

### 24-A それぞれの英単語の意味に最も当てはまる日本語を選びましょう。

1) **appreciation** [əpriːʃiéɪʃən]

2) **caterer** [kéɪtərər]

3) **contractor** [kάːntræktər]

4) **decade** [dékeɪd]

5) **duty** [d(j)úːti]

6) **founder** [fáʊndər]

7) **personnel** [pə̀ːrsənél]

8) **critic** [krítɪk]

9) **departure** [dɪpάːrtʃər]

10) **destination** [dèstənéɪʃən]

11) **district** [dístrɪkt]

12) **executive** [ɪgzékjətɪv]

13) **inquiry** [ínkwəri]

14) **medication** [mèdəkéɪʃən]

15) **spokesperson** [spóʊkspə̀ːrsn]

16) **statement** [stéɪtmənt]

17) **tenant** [ténənt]

18) **venue** [vénjuː]

19) **commitment** [kəmítmənt]

20) **competition** [kὰːmpətíʃən]

| | | | |
|---|---|---|---|
| 行き先 | 開催場所 | 感謝 | 競争 |
| ケータリング業者 | 工事請負業者 | 広報担当者 | 十年間 |
| 重役 | 出発 | 職務 | スタッフ |
| 創設者 | 地区 | 賃借人 | 問い合わせ |
| 批評家 | 明細書 | 薬剤 | 約束 |

## 24-B
音声を聴き、英文の空所にあてはまる単語を入れ、その単語に該当する日本語を○で囲みましょう。
（単語は必要に応じて変化させましょう。）

**143**

1. The food ( critic ) was impressed with the restaurant's cuisine.
   その料理批評家はそのレストランの料理に感銘を受けた。

2. We've been producing vehicles with attractive designs for ( decades ).
   当社は人の目を引き付けるデザインの車を数十年間製造してきた。

3. Laura's ideal vacation ( destination ) is Hawaii.
   ローラの理想の休暇の行き先はハワイだ。

4. As ( founder ) of the firm, he has always tried to develop competitive products.
   会社の創設者として、彼は常に他社に負けない製品を開発しようとしてきた。

5. The employees' responses to the food prepared by the ( caterer ) were positive.
   そのケータリング業者が準備した料理への従業員たちの反応は好意的だった。

**144**

6. Emily expressed ( appreciation ) to the attendees of the fund-raising event.
   エミリーは資金集めのイベントの出席者に感謝を表現した。

7. The administrative ( duties ) that Jim had taken over were challenging.
   ジムが引き継いだ管理職務は大変だがやりがいがあった。

8. Mike delayed the time of ( departure ) due to his dental appointment.
   マイクは歯科の予約のために出発時間を遅らせた。

9. The home renovation ( contractor ) uses durable building materials.
   その家屋リフォーム工事請負業者は耐久性のある建材を使っている。

10. The company is looking for senior technical ( personnel ).
    その会社は上級技術スタッフを探している。

---

- ☐ appreciation ☐ critic ☐ destination ☐ personnel
- ☐ caterer ☐ decade ☐ duty
- ☐ contractor ☐ departure ☐ founder

## 24-C

音声を聴き、英文の空所にあてはまる単語を入れ、その単語に該当する日本語を○で囲みましょう。
（単語は必要に応じて変化させましょう。）

1. Facing strong (　　　　　), the company decided to offer reduced prices.
   激しい競争に直面して、その会社は割引料金を提供することを決めた。

2. Your billing (　　　　　) can be viewed on our website.
   お客さまの請求明細書は当社のウェブサイトでご覧いただけます。

3. The city is eager to attract tourists to its historic (　　　　　).
   その市は観光客を市の史跡地区に呼び込むことに熱心だ。

4. The prospective mayor made a (　　　　　) to rebuild the city.
   その市長候補は市を再建する約束をした。

5. The (　　　　　) signed an extended contract with the owner.
   その賃借人は所有者との延長契約書に署名をした。

6. The company (　　　　　) said that its website was secure from any possible cyber-attacks.
   その会社の広報担当者は社のウェブサイトは起こりうるいかなるサイバー攻撃からも安全だと言った。

7. James' initial response to the guest's (　　　　　) was judged to be appropriate.
   宿泊客からの問い合わせへのジェイムズの初動対応は適切だと評価された。

8. Anne was confident that she had developed an effective new (　　　　　).
   アンは効果的な新しい薬剤開発したという自信があった。

9. Kyoto is a suitable (　　　　　) for an international conference.
   京都は国際会議にふさわしい開催場所だ。

10. The marketing (　　　　　) proposed launching a new high-quality food brand.
    市場戦略担当の重役は新しい高級食品ブランドを立ち上げることを提案した。

---

| ☐ commitment | ☐ executive | ☐ spokesperson | ☐ venue |
| ☐ competition | ☐ inquiry | ☐ statement | |
| ☐ district | ☐ medication | ☐ tenant | |

## 24-D

● それぞれの語の類義語を、この UNIT の見出し語から選びましょう。

1) promise _____
2) region _____
3) reviewer _____
4) task _____
5) thanks _____

● それぞれの語の動詞形を書きましょう。

1) competition _____
2) departure _____
3) founder _____
4) inquiry _____
5) statement _____

## 24-E

空所に入る最も適切な語を選びましょう。ただし、それぞれの語の意味はこの UNIT で取り扱ったものとします。

1. Fred confirmed the food menu for the company picnic with the ------.

   (A) appreciation　　(B) caterer　　(C) departure　　(D) district

2. Taro felt that Osaka would be the ideal ------ for the next Olympics.

   (A) competition　　(B) executive　　(C) personnel　　(D) venue

3. The real estate agency showed some commercial properties to a prospective ------.

   (A) decade　　(B) duty　　(C) inquiry　　(D) tenant

4. Lucy received instructions from the pharmacist on how to take the ------.

   (A) contractor　　(B) critic　　(C) medication　　(D) statement

5. The mayor wants the city's hot spring resort to be a popular ------.

   (A) commitment　　(B) destination　　(C) founder　　(D) spokesperson

# UNIT 25
## 動詞 7

**25-A** それぞれの英単語の意味に最も当てはまる日本語を選びましょう。

1) **demonstrate** [démənstrèɪt]

2) **emphasize** [émfəsàɪz]

3) **evaluate** [ɪvæljuèɪt]

4) **exceed** [ɪksíːd]

5) **expire** [ɪkspáɪər]

6) **monitor** [máːnətər]

7) **operate** [áːpərèɪt]

8) **predict** [prɪdíkt]

9) **supervise** [súːpərvàɪz]

10) **negotiate** [nəgóʊʃièɪt]

11) **operate** [áːpərèɪt]

12) **raise** [réɪz]

13) **recognize** [rékəgnàɪz]

14) **review** [rɪvjúː]

15) **enclose** [ɪnklóʊz]

16) **promote** [prəmóʊt]

17) **reflect** [rɪflékt]

18) **restore** [rɪstóːr]

19) **forward** [fóːrwərd]

20) **transfer** [trænsfóːr]

---

| | | | |
|---|---|---|---|
| 集める [お金を] | 営業する | 監視する | 監督する |
| 期限が切れる | 強調する | 交渉して取り決める | 超える |
| 実演する | 修復する | 昇進させる | 操作する |
| 転勤する | 転送する | 同封する | 反映する |
| 批評する [論評する] | 評価する [査定する] | 表彰する | 予測する |

## 25-B
音声を聴き、英文の空所にあてはまる単語を入れ、その単語に該当する日本語を○で囲みましょう。
（単語は必要に応じて変化させましょう。）

1. The company founder ( ) the importance of competition between departments.
   その会社の創設者は部署間での競争の重要性を強調した。

2. Bill ( ) a new agreement with the contractor.
   ビルはその請負業者と新しい契約を交渉して取り決めた。

3. The sales executive accurately ( ) sales of the new laptop.
   その販売担当重役は新しいノートパソコンの売上を正確に予測した。

4. Mike ( ) the new software installation procedure to all personnel.
   マイクは新しいソフトウェアのインストールの手順をスタッフ全員に実演した。

5. The cameras ( ) the airport departure lobby at all times.
   カメラが空港の出発ロビーを常時監視している。

6. The number of customer inquiries ( ) 100 a day.
   顧客からの問い合わせ件数が1日に100件を超えた。

7. One of Sally's duties is to ( ) the laboratory personnel.
   サリーの職務のひとつは研究所のスタッフを監督することだ。

8. The contract with the tenant ( ) next month.
   その賃借人との契約は来月に期限が切れる。

9. The new medication is highly ( ) by a lot of doctors.
   その新薬は多くの医師に高く評価されている。

10. I've been ( ) these factory machines for a decade.
    私は10年間ずっとこれらの工場の機械を操作してきた。

---

☐ demonstrate　　☐ exceed　　☐ negotiate　　☐ supervise
☐ emphasize　　　☐ expire　　☐ operate　　　
☐ evaluate　　　　☐ monitor　　☐ predict

## 25-C

音声を聴き、英文の空所にあてはまる単語を入れ、その単語に該当する日本語を◯で囲みましょう。
（単語は必要に応じて変化させましょう。）

1. The company ( recognized ) Ellen for her efforts to develop the new software.
   その会社は新しいソフトウェアを開発しようとする努力に対してエレンを表彰した。

2. That city's new policies ( reflect ) the mayor's commitments to the citizens.
   その市の新しい政策には市長の市民との約束が反映されている。

3. Linda is ( transferring ) to the Nagoya branch next month.
   リンダは来月名古屋支店に転勤する予定だ。

4. David was ( promoted ) to general manager of the city's southern district.
   デイビッドは市の南部地区の統括マネジャーに昇進した。

5. The local hikers appreciated the city's decision to ( restore ) the trail.
   地元のハイカーたちは登山道を修復するという市の決定をありがたく思った。

6. Please find ( enclosed ) your credit card statement.
   お客さまのクレジットカードの明細書を同封いたしました。

7. George ( forwarded ) the convention schedule to his colleague at the venue.
   ジョージはその大会の予定表を開催場所にいる同僚に転送した。

8. According to the spokesperson, the company ( raised ) enough funds for renovating their headquarters.
   広報担当者によれば、社は本社をリフォームする十分な資金を集めたそうだ。

9. That caterer ( operates ) in more than 10 cities.
   そのケータリング業者は10以上の市で営業している。

10. The food critic ( reviewed ) some long-established restaurants in the city.
    その料理評論家はその市のいくつかの老舗レストランを批評した。

---

| ☐ enclose | ☐ promote | ☐ reflect | ☐ transfer |
| ☐ forward | ☐ raise | ☐ restore | |
| ☐ operate | ☐ recognize | ☐ review | |

## 25-D

● それぞれの語の類義語を、このUNITの見出し語から選びましょう。

1) advance _____
2) anticipate _____
3) assess _____
4) relocate _____
5) work _____

● それぞれの語の名詞形を書きましょう。

1) demonstrate _____
2) emphasize _____
3) negotiate _____
4) recognize _____
5) restore _____

## 25-E

空所に入る最も適切な語を選びましょう。ただし、それぞれの語の意味はこのUNITで取り扱ったものとします。

1. Would you ------ the travel itinerary to my private email address?

    (A) emphasize　　(B) forward　　(C) monitor　　(D) restore

2. Do you know when the warranty on the fridge will ------?

    (A) expire　　(B) negotiate　　(C) operate　　(D) transfer

3. John's work in the accounting firm will probably ------ his associates' expectations.

    (A) evaluate　　(B) exceed　　(C) recognize　　(D) supervise

4. The company held the event in order to ------ money to donate to charities.

    (A) demonstrate　　(B) predict　　(C) raise　　(D) review

5. Could you ------ a letter of recommendation with your résumé?

    (A) enclose　　(B) operate　　(C) promote　　(D) reflect

# UNIT 26
## 名詞 14

**26-A** それぞれの英単語の意味に最も当てはまる日本語を選びましょう。

1) **defect** [díːfekt]

2) **expertise** [èkspərtíːz]

3) **fare** [féər]

4) **organizer** [ɔ́ːrgənàɪzər]

5) **preference** [préfərəns]

6) **prescription** [prɪskrípʃən]

7) **progress** [práːgres]

8) **questionnaire** [kwèstʃənéər]

9) **retailer** [ríːtèɪlər]

10) **review** [rɪvjúː]

11) **sculpture** [skʌ́lptʃər]

12) **statement** [stéɪtmənt]

13) **terms** [tə́ːrmz]

14) **administrator** [ədmínəstrèɪtər]

15) **deal** [díːl]

16) **directory** [dəréktəri]

17) **landmark** [lǽndmɑːrk]

18) **priority** [praɪɔ́(ː)rəti]

19) **receptionist** [rɪsépʃənɪst]

20) **reward** [rɪwɔ́ːrd]

---

| | | | |
|---|---|---|---|
| アンケート | 受付係 | 運賃 | 管理者 [運営をする人] |
| 欠陥 | 小売業者 | 好み | 主催者 [準備をする人] |
| 条件 | 処方箋 | 進行 | 声明 |
| 専門知識 | 彫像 | 取引 | 報酬 |
| 見直し | 名所旧跡 | 名簿 | 優先事項 |

UNIT 26／名詞 14  107

## 26-B
音声を聴き、英文の空所にあてはまる単語を入れ、その単語に該当する日本語を○で囲みましょう。
（単語は必要に応じて変化させましょう。）

1. Ray has the necessary ( **expertise** ) to review computer products.
   レイにはコンピュータ製品を批評するのに必要な専門知識がある。

2. They had to conduct a full ( **review** ) of the proposal budget.
   彼らは予算案の全面的な見直しをしなければならなかった。

3. Mary's evaluation of her subordinates is currently in ( **progress** ).
   メアリによる部下の評価は現在進行中だ。

4. The event ( **organizers** ) raised money for some charities.
   イベントの主催者たちは慈善団体のためにお金を集めた。

5. The number of responses to the ( **questionnaire** ) exceeded 10,000.
   そのアンケートへの回答数は1万を超えた。

6. The company's clothing line reflects the ( **preferences** ) of young people.
   その会社の衣料品は若者の好みを反映している。

7. The grocery ( **retailer** ) is operating in a temporary store.
   その食料雑貨小売業者は仮店舗で営業中だ。

8. They found more ( **defects** ) in the machine than predicted.
   彼らは予測されていたよりも多くその機械の欠陥を見つけた。

9. The city's subway ( **fares** ) were raised significantly.
   その市の地下鉄の運賃が大幅に値上げされた。

10. The ( **prescription** ) for the medicine was no longer valid.
    その薬の処方箋はもう期限が切れていた。

---

| ☐ defect | ☐ organizer | ☐ progress | ☐ review |
| ☐ expertise | ☐ preference | ☐ questionnaire | |
| ☐ fare | ☐ prescription | ☐ retailer | |

## 26-C

音声を聴き、英文の空所にあてはまる単語を入れ、その単語に該当する日本語を○で囲みましょう。
（単語は必要に応じて変化させましょう。）

1. Cathy was recognized for her thirty-year service as a (　　　　) at the company.
   キャシーは受付係として会社勤続30年で表彰された。

2. In the (　　　　), the CEO emphasized the project's importance.
   声明の中で、最高経営責任者はそのプロジェクトの重要性を強調した。

3. What is the top (　　　　) in this business deal?
   今回の商取引において最優先事項はどのようなことですか。

4. Jane can refuse to transfer under her (　　　　) of employment.
   ジェインは彼女の雇用条件の下では転勤を拒否することが可能だ。

5. I've enclosed a (　　　　) of those people who donated money.
   お金を寄付していただいた方々の名簿を同封しております。

6. Jim forwarded the details of the (　　　　) to his supervisor.
   ジムは取引の詳細を上司に転送した。

7. Susie was promoted to chief system (　　　　).
   スージーは主任システム管理者に昇進した。

8. Tom operated the cameras monitoring (　　　　) in the exhibition room.
   トムは展示室の彫像を監視するカメラを操作した。

9. Kate deserves a (　　　　) for her efforts in developing the new software.
   新しいソフトウェアを開発するケイトの努力は報酬に値する。

10. The city council decided to restore the (　　　　) to its original state.
    市議会はその名所旧跡を元の状態に修復することに決めた。

---

- ☐ administrator
- ☐ landmark
- ☐ reward
- ☐ terms
- ☐ deal
- ☐ priority
- ☐ sculpture
- ☐ directory
- ☐ receptionist
- ☐ statement

## 26-D

● それぞれの語の類義語を、この UNIT の見出し語から選びましょう。

1) conditions _____
2) liking _____
3) list _____
4) statue _____
5) survey _____

● それぞれの語の形容詞形を書きましょう。

1) administrator _____
2) defect _____
3) priority _____
4) progress _____
5) retailer _____

## 26-E

空所に入る最も適切な語を選びましょう。ただし、それぞれの語の意味はこの UNIT で取り扱ったものとします。

1. The summer rock festival ------ urged the audience to drink enough water.

    (A) directory　　(B) organizer　　(C) questionnaire　　(D) retailer

2. We are looking for an individual with ------ in marketing.

    (A) expertise　　(B) prescription　　(C) priority　　(D) terms

3. How much is the round-trip train ------ from Osaka to Kyoto?

    (A) administrator　　(B) fare　　(C) progress　　(D) sculpture

4. The castle is a historic ------ of the city and is worth visiting.

    (A) landmark　　(B) preference　　(C) review　　(D) statement

5. Jack received a ------ for his contribution to the development of the new project.

    (A) deal　　(B) defect　　(C) receptionist　　(D) reward

# UNIT 27
## 形容詞 4

**27-A** それぞれの英単語の意味に最も当てはまる日本語を選びましょう。

1) **culinary** [kʌ́lənèri]

2) **eligible** [élədʒəbl]

3) **flexible** [fléksəbl]

4) **former** [fɔ́ːrmər]

5) **generous** [dʒénərəs]

6) **individual** [ìndəvídʒuəl]

7) **leading** [líːdɪŋ]

8) **postal** [póʊstl]

9) **significant** [sɪɡnífɪkənt]

10) **urgent** [ə́ːrdʒənt]

11) **alternate** [ɔ́ːltərnət]

12) **enthusiastic** [ɪnθ(j)ùːziǽstɪk]

13) **exclusive** [ɪksklúːsɪv]

14) **reasonable** [ríːznəbl]

15) **relevant** [réləvənt]

16) **sustainable** [səstéɪnəbl]

17) **appropriate** [əpróʊpriət]

18) **critical** [krítɪkl]

19) **defective** [dɪféktɪv]

20) **resistant** [rɪzístənt]

---

| 以前の | かなりの | 代わりの | 関連した |
| 気前の良い | 緊急の | 欠陥のある | 個々の |
| 資格がある | 持続可能な | 主要な | 耐性がある |
| 適切な | 手ごろな | 独占的な | とても重要な |
| 熱心な | 融通の利く | 郵便の | 料理の |

## 27-B
音声を聴き、英文の空所にあてはまる単語を入れ、その単語に該当する日本語を○で囲みましょう。
（単語は必要に応じて変化させましょう。）

1. In the city, residents over 65 are ( ) for free public transportation.
   その市では 65 歳以上の住民は公共交通機関が無料の資格がある。

2. The board held an ( ) meeting to discuss the product defect.
   役員たちはその製品の欠陥について話し合うために緊急の会議を開いた。

3. The ( ) workers' performance deserved a reward.
   その郵便局員たちの仕事ぶりは報酬に値した。

4. James received instructions to review each ( ) survey response.
   ジェイムズは個々の調査回答を見直すよう指示を受けた。

5. The law firm made the receptionists' work shifts more ( ).
   その法律事務所は受付係の仕事のシフトをより融通の利くものにした。

6. The city's tourism industry has made ( ) progress.
   市の観光業はかなりの進展をしてきた。

7. Laura is an instructor with extensive ( ) skills and experience.
   ローラは幅広い料理の技術と経験がある講師だ。

8. The event organizers received ( ) financial support from the sponsor.
   イベント主催者たちはそのスポンサーから気前の良い財政面の援助を受けた。

9. The country's ( ) airlines raised their fares.
   その国の主要な航空会社が運賃を値上げした。

10. The retailer took over the store from the ( ) owner.
    その小売業者は以前のオーナーから店を引き継いだ。

| ☐ culinary | ☐ former | ☐ leading | ☐ urgent |
| --- | --- | --- | --- |
| ☐ eligible | ☐ generous | ☐ postal | |
| ☐ flexible | ☐ individual | ☐ significant | |

## 27-C

音声を聴き、英文の空所にあてはまる単語を入れ、その単語に該当する日本語を◯で囲みましょう。
（単語は必要に応じて変化させましょう。）

1. It's ( ) that we sign the agreement on favorable terms.
   われわれは有利な条件で契約を結ぶことがとても重要だ。

2. Our line of glassware is highly ( ) to heat.
   当社のガラス食器製品は熱に対して非常に耐性がある。

3. The museum purchased several sculptures at ( ) prices.
   その美術館は手ごろな価格で数点の彫像を購入した。

4. Fred had to arrange ( ) transportation because of flight cancellations.
   欠航のため、フレッドは代わりの交通手段を手配しなければならなかった。

5. The company stated that it would develop environmentally ( ) products.
   その会社は環境的に持続可能な商品を開発することを明言した。

6. Our store replaces any ( ) items promptly.
   当店は欠陥のある商品は速やかに交換させていただきます。

7. The vendor is ( ) about finalizing a deal with the manufacturer.
   その供給業者はそのメーカーとの取引をまとめることに熱心だ。

8. The road isn't ( ) for bike commuters due to the heavy traffic.
   その道路は交通量が多いので自転車通勤の人には適切ではない。

9. The journalist had an ( ) interview with the company CEO.
   その報道記者はその会社の最高経営責任者と独占インタヴューを行った。

10. Mike gathered the ( ) materials to write his article.
    マイクは記事を書くために関連した資料を集めた。

---

| ☐ alternate | ☐ defective | ☐ reasonable | ☐ sustainable |
|---|---|---|---|
| ☐ appropriate | ☐ enthusiastic | ☐ relevant | |
| ☐ critical | ☐ exclusive | ☐ resistant | |

UNIT 27／形容詞4

## 27-D

● それぞれの語の類義語を、このUNITの見出し語から選びましょう。

1) eager _____
2) qualified _____
3) suitable _____
4) top _____
5) vital _____

● それぞれの語の名詞形を書きましょう。

1) defective _____
2) flexible _____
3) generous _____
4) reasonable _____
5) significant _____

## 27-E

空所に入る最も適切な語を選びましょう。ただし、それぞれの語の意味はこのUNITで取り扱ったものとします。

1. The store specializes in high-quality ------ utensils and equipment.

   (A) culinary　　(B) eligible　　(C) significant　　(D) urgent

2. The residents in the district have two ------ deliveries on weekdays.

   (A) critical　　(B) former　　(C) individual　　(D) postal

3. The manufacturer's glasses lenses are ------ to scratches.

   (A) appropriate　　(B) leading　　(C) reasonable　　(D) resistant

4. The front-page story is ------ to that newspaper.

   (A) alternate　　(B) exclusive　　(C) flexible　　(D) sustainable

5. We're looking for a person with ------ job experience for the position.

   (A) defective　　(B) enthusiastic　　(C) generous　　(D) relevant

# UNIT 28
## 名詞 15

**28-A** それぞれの英単語の意味に最も当てはまる日本語を選びましょう。

🎧 165
1) **individual** [ìndəvídʒuəl]
2) **publicity** [pʌblísəti]
3) **qualification** [kwàːləfɪkéɪʃən]
4) **recipient** [rɪsípiənt]
5) **reimbursement** [rìːɪmbə́ːrsmənt]
6) **specifications** [spèsəfɪkéɪʃənz]
7) **transaction** [trænsǽkʃən]
8) **transition** [trænzíʃən]
9) **voucher** [váʊtʃər]
10) **architecture** [áːrkətektʃər]

🎧 166
11) **auditorium** [ɔ̀ːdətɔ́ːriəm]
12) **employer** [ɪmplɔ́ɪər]
13) **enrollment** [ɪnróʊlmənt]
14) **envelope** [énvəlòʊp]
15) **extension** [ɪksténʃən]
16) **guidelines** [gáɪdlàɪnz]
17) **minutes** [mínəts]
18) **nutrition** [n(j)u(ː)tríʃən]
19) **overtime** [óʊvərtàɪm]
20) **wildlife** [wáɪldlàɪf]

| | | | |
|---|---|---|---|
| 移行 | 受取人 | 栄養 | ガイドライン |
| 議事録 | クーポン券 | 建築 | 講堂 |
| 雇用主 | 残業 | 資格 | 仕様（書） |
| 宣伝広報 | 登録（数） | 取引 | 内線 |
| 払い戻し | 人 | 封筒 | 野生生物 |

## 28-B
音声を聴き、英文の空所にあてはまる単語を入れ、その単語に該当する日本語を○で囲みましょう。
（単語は必要に応じて変化させましょう。）

🎧167

1. The company completed a (　　　　　　) with the wholesaler.
   その会社は卸売業者と取引を完了した。

2. The decision to make that actor the (　　　　　　) of the award was appropriate.
   その俳優をその賞の受賞者にする決定は適切だった。

3. Our members are eligible to receive discount (　　　　　　).
   当会員は割引クーポン券を受け取る資格がある。

4. The additional (　　　　　　) led to a significant increase in sales.
   その追加の宣伝広報がかなりの売上増加につながった。

5. Judging from the (　　　　　　), this laptop should be quite shock resistant.
   仕様書から判断すると、このノートパソコンは衝撃に対してかなり耐性があるはずだ。

🎧168

6. The customer asked for (　　　　　　) for the defective product.
   その顧客は欠陥のある商品への払い戻しを求めた。

7. A smooth (　　　　　　) to our new website is critical.
   当社の新しいウェブサイトへのスムースな移行がとても重要だ。

8. That company focuses on (　　　　　　) which uses sustainable building materials.
   その会社は持続可能な建築材を用いる建築に重点をおいている。

9. We are seeking an enthusiastic (　　　　　　) who is flexible regarding work time.
   われわれは勤務時間に融通が利く熱心な人を探しています。

10. Lucy has several (　　　　　　) that are relevant to her current job.
    ルーシーは現在の仕事に関連した多くの資格を持っている。

---

| ☐ architecture | ☐ qualification | ☐ specifications | ☐ voucher |
| ☐ individual | ☐ recipient | ☐ transaction | |
| ☐ publicity | ☐ reimbursement | ☐ transition | |

## 28-C

音声を聴き、英文の空所にあてはまる単語を入れ、その単語に該当する日本語を○で囲みましょう。
（単語は必要に応じて変化させましょう。）

1. The rangers looked for an alternate means of protecting the park's ( wildlife ).
   国立公園管理者たちはその公園の野生生物を保護する別の手段を探した。

2. Sally completed her ( enrollment ) in the workshop run by a well-known culinary expert.
   サリーは著名な料理専門家が運営する講習会への登録を終えた。

3. Ellen played a leading role in revising the staff ( guidelines ).
   エレンは職員向けガイドラインを見直すことに主要な役割を果たした。

4. I've attached a letter of recommendation from my former ( employer ).
   私の以前の雇用主からの推薦状を同封いたしました。

5. Matt got adequate ( nutrition ) from his diet.
   マットは毎日の食事で十分な栄養を取った。

6. Susie asked the operator to put her through to ( extension ) 007.
   スージーは交換手に内線 007 番につないでもらった。

7. Linda worked ( overtime ) to finish the exclusive interview article with the CEO.
   リンダはその最高経営責任者との独占インタビュー記事を仕上げるために残業をした。

8. Bill ordered a large quantity of ( envelopes ) at a reasonable price.
   ビルは手ごろな価格の封筒を大量に注文した。

9. A generous donation made the renovation of the ( auditorium ) possible.
   寛大な寄付のおかげでその講堂のリフォームが可能になった。

10. Urgent business prevented David from taking the ( minutes ) of the meeting.
    急用のためにデイビッドはその会議の議事録を取ることができなかった。

---

| ☐ auditorium | ☐ envelope | ☐ minutes | ☐ wildlife |
| ☐ employer | ☐ extension | ☐ nutrition | |
| ☐ enrollment | ☐ guidelines | ☐ overtime | |

## 28-D

● それぞれの語の類義語を、この UNIT の見出し語から選びましょう。

1) change _____
2) coupon _____
3) deal _____
4) person _____
5) receiver _____

● それぞれの語の動詞形を書きましょう。

1) enrollment _____
2) extension _____
3) publicity _____
4) qualification _____
5) reimbursement _____

## 28-E

空所に入る最も適切な語を選びましょう。ただし、それぞれの語の意味はこの UNIT で取り扱ったものとします。

1. Please send back the survey form in the enclosed ------.

    (A) enrollment    (B) envelope    (C) qualification    (D) voucher

2. George entered the ------ of the meeting into the computer.

    (A) individual    (B) minutes    (C) overtime    (D) specifications

3. The lecture by the well-known architect was delivered in the ------.

    (A) auditorium    (B) extension    (C) reimbursement    (D) transition

4. Our school meals provide excellent ------ for students.

    (A) employer    (B) nutrition    (C) publicity    (D) recipient

5. You can see a rich variety of ------ on the safari tour.

    (A) architecture    (B) guidelines    (C) transaction    (D) wildlife

# UNIT 29
## 副詞

**29-A** それぞれの英単語の意味に最も当てはまる日本語を選びましょう。

🎧 171

1) **currently** [ká:rəntli]

2) **actually** [ǽktʃuəli]

3) **previously** [prí:viəsli]

4) **unfortunately** [ʌnfɔ́:rtʃənətli]

5) **highly** [háɪli]

6) **properly** [prá:pərli]

7) **definitely** [défənətli]

8) **nearly** [níərli]

9) **regularly** [régjələrli]

10) **extremely** [ɪkstrí:mli]

🎧 172

11) **approximately** [əprá:ksəmətli]

12) **exactly** [ɪgzǽktli]

13) **eventually** [ɪvéntʃuəli]

14) **shortly** [ʃɔ́:rtli]

15) **tentatively** [téntətɪvli]

16) **thoroughly** [θə́:rouli]

17) **consistently** [kənsístəntli]

18) **relatively** [rélətɪvli]

19) **accurately** [ǽkjərətli]

20) **consequently** [ká:nsəkwèntli]

---

| | | | |
|---|---|---|---|
| 以前に | おおよそ [その前後] | 仮に | 結局は [ついにやっと] |
| 現在 | 残念ながら | 実は | 首尾一貫して |
| 正確に [ぴったりの] | 正確に [まちがいのない] | 絶対に | その結果 [したがって] |
| 定期的に | 適切に | 徹底的に | 比較的 |
| 非常に [水準が高い] | 非常に [程度が大きい] | ほぼ [もう少しで] | まもなく |

## 29-B
音声を聴き、英文の空所にあてはまる単語を入れ、その単語に該当する日本語を○で囲みましょう。
（単語は必要に応じて変化させましょう。）

🎧 173

1. It's ( extremely ) important to complete the transition to the new computer system.
新しいコンピュータシステムへの移行を完了させることが非常に大切だ。

2. Nancy is ( highly ) respected for having so many technical qualifications.
ナンシーはとても多くの技術的な資格を持っていることで非常に尊敬されている。

3. That supplier is reliable so you should ( definitely ) make a deal with them.
その供給業者は信頼できるので、あなたは絶対に取引をするべきだ。

4. The ranger hadn't ( previously ) seen any wildlife in the area.
その国立公園管理者はそのエリアでは以前に野生生物をまったく見かけたことがなかった。

5. The safety guidelines for workers at the factory are ( regularly ) updated.
その工場での従業員用の安全に関するガイドラインは定期的に更新される。

🎧 174

6. ( Actually ), the successful product was given very little publicity.
実はそのヒット商品はほとんど宣伝広報をされなかった。

7. ( Unfortunately ), Mary had to work overtime yesterday.
残念ながらメアリは昨日残業をしなければならなかった。

8. ( Nearly ) 10 percent of people aren't at home when packages are delivered.
荷物の配達時に、ほぼ10パーセントの人が在宅していない。

9. We are ( currently ) looking for a creative individual to help with advertising.
当社は現在広告業務で助けとなるクリエイティブな人材を求めている。

10. The architecture firm has a good reputation because they do things ( properly ).
その建築事務所は仕事を適切に行なうので評判が良い。

---

| ☐ actually | ☐ extremely | ☐ previously | ☐ unfortunately |
| ☐ currently | ☐ highly | ☐ properly | |
| ☐ definitely | ☐ nearly | ☐ regularly | |

## 29-C

音声を聴き、英文の空所にあてはまる単語を入れ、その単語に該当する日本語を○で囲みましょう。
（単語は必要に応じて変化させましょう。）

1. Our restaurant has ( consistently ) focused on serving nutritious food.
   当レストランは首尾一貫して栄養豊富な料理を提供することに重点をおいてきました。

2. The number of students enrolled in the course is ( approximately ) 100.
   その講座に登録している学生数はおおよそ100名だ。

3. The company's new marketing strategy ( accurately ) reflects the views of the management.
   その会社の新しい市場戦略は経営陣の意見を正確に反映している。

4. Jane ( thoroughly ) analyzed the results of her market research.
   ジェインは市場調査の結果を徹底的に分析した。

5. The credit card company ( eventually ) provided a reimbursement for the incorrect charges.
   結局そのクレジットカード会社は間違った請求への払い戻しを行った。

6. The vouchers were distributed and ( consequently ) the shop's sales increased.
   クーポン券が配布され、その結果その店の売り上げが増えた。

7. Restoration work on the building will be completed ( shortly ).
   建物の復旧作業はまもなく完了します。

8. The personnel manager ( tentatively ) assigned the interns to each department.
   人事部長は研修生を各部署に仮に割り当てた。

9. Office supplies are ( relatively ) inexpensive at the store.
   事務用品はその店が比較的安い。

10. Could you tell me ( exactly ) what my new job will involve?
    私の新しい仕事にはどのようなことが伴うのか正確に教えていただけますか。

---

☐ accurately　☐ consistently　☐ relatively　☐ thoroughly
☐ approximately　☐ eventually　☐ shortly
☐ consequently　☐ exactly　☐ tentatively

## 29-D

● それぞれの語の類義語を、このUNITの見出し語から選びましょう。

1) about _____
2) almost _____
3) before _____
4) comparatively _____
5) finally _____
6) now _____
7) soon _____
8) suitably _____
9) therefore _____
10) unluckily _____

## 29-E

空所に入る最も適切な語を選びましょう。ただし、それぞれの語の意味はこのUNITで取り扱ったものとします。

**1.** They ------ agreed to Susie's proposal at this morning's meeting.

   (A) previously     (B) regularly     (C) relatively     (D) tentatively

**2.** ------, I've already seen that movie with my colleagues.

   (A) Actually     (B) Definitely     (C) Eventually     (D) Nearly

**3.** We're ------ pleased to announce the completion of our new office building.

   (A) accurately     (B) consequently     (C) extremely     (D) properly

**4.** Ray spent half a day ------ cleaning the exterior of his house yesterday.

   (A) exactly     (B) highly     (C) shortly     (D) thoroughly

**5.** We've ------ maintained the low price of the computer since we launched it.

   (A) approximately     (B) consistently     (C) currently     (D) unfortunately

# UNIT 30
## 熟語・構文 2

**30-A** それぞれの英熟語・英語構文の意味に最も当てはまる日本語を選びましょう。

1) hand out
2) in person
3) be likely to 不定詞
4) drop off
5) Please note that 節
6) prior to 名詞
7) come up with
8) feel free to 不定詞
9) in time (for)
10) on display

11) take over
12) depend on
13) as of
14) be looking to 不定詞
15) go over
16) result in
17) be honored to 不定詞
18) on behalf of
19) run out of
20) be subject to 名詞

---

| | | | |
|---|---|---|---|
| 遠慮なく…する | 思いつく | 結果として…になる | …しそうである |
| …しだいである | …しようと思っている | 対面で | 陳列されて |
| 使い果たす | 届ける | …にご注意ください | …の時点で |
| …の場合がある | …の前に | 配布する | 引き継ぐ |
| 間に合って | 綿密に調べる | …を光栄に思う | …を代表して |

## 30-B
音声を聴き、英文の空欄にあてはまる語句を入れ、その語句に該当する日本語を○で囲みましょう。
（語句中の単語は必要に応じて変化させましょう。）

1. Emily carefully measured the sofa ( prior to ) purchasing it.
   エミリーはソファーを購入する前に慎重にその寸法を測った。

2. Would you ( drop off ) the document at the marketing department?
   その書類をマーケティング部に届けてもらえますか。

3. The gallery always has beautiful paintings ( on display ).
   その画廊はいつも美しい絵画を陳列している。

4. Eventually, Tom ( is likely to ) succeed as an entrepreneur.
   ゆくゆくはトムは起業家として成功しそうだ。

5. Please ( feel free to ) contact me if you have any questions.
   ご質問がある場合にはどうぞ遠慮なく私にご連絡ください。

6. ( Please note that ) the fitness room is currently closed.
   フィットネスルームは現在閉鎖中であることにご注意ください。

7. Cathy ( handed out ) copies of the agenda at the board meeting.
   キャシーは役員会議で議題の用紙を配布した。

8. We thought we would definitely be late, but we arrived just ( in time ).
   われわれは絶対に遅刻すると思ったが、ちょうど間に合って到着した。

9. Ray regularly met with his clients ( in person ).
   レイは定期的に対面で顧客に会った。

10. Jack eventually ( came up with ) a great marketing idea.
    ジャックはすばらしい市場戦略のアイデアをついに思いついた。

---

- ☐ **be likely to** 不定詞　☐ **feel free to** 不定詞　☐ **in time (for)**　☐ **prior to** 名詞
- ☐ **come up with**　☐ **hand out**　☐ **on display**
- ☐ **drop off**　☐ **in person**　☐ **Please note that** 節

## 30-e

音声を聴き、英文の空欄にあてはまる語句を入れ、その語句に該当する日本語を○で囲みましょう。
（語句中の単語は必要に応じて変化させましょう。）

1. We're ( ) open another branch in the city next year.
   われわれは来年市内にもうひとつ支店をオープンしようと思っている。

2. Whether our proposal will be accepted ( ) our presentation.
   われわれの案が採用されるかどうかはわれわれのプレゼンしだいだ。

3. We're ( ) paper for the copier.
   われわれはコピー機の用紙を使い果たしそうだ。

4. Actually, Laura helped me to ( ) the contract.
   実は、ローラが私がその契約書を綿密に調べることを手伝ってくれた。

5. Matt ( ) be recognized for his contributions to that project.
   マットはそのプロジェクトへの貢献に対して表彰されたことを光栄に思っている。

6. The prices ( ) change without notice.
   価格は予告なく変更になる場合があります。

7. James negotiated with the management ( ) approximately 100 employees.
   ジェイムズはおおよそ100名の従業員を代表して経営陣と交渉した。

8. ( ) today, that film has received relatively positive reviews from movie critics.
   本日の時点で、その映画は映画評論家から比較的好意的な批評を得ている。

9. Unfortunately, our shortage of staff ( ) lower sales.
   残念なことに、人手不足が結果として当社の売上の減少になった。

10. Kate ( ) the duties of the former manager.
    ケイトは前任のマネジャーの職務を引き継いだ。

---

| ☐ as of | ☐ be subject to 名詞 | ☐ depend on | ☐ result in |
| ☐ be honored to 不定詞 | | ☐ go over | ☐ run out of |
| ☐ be looking to 不定詞 | | ☐ on behalf of | ☐ take over |

# 30-D

● この Unit で取り扱っている意味の熟語・構文の類義表現になるように、指定された出だしの文字で始まる1語を空所に書き込みましょう。ただし、空所の前に⇔の記号がある場合には反意表現になるようにしましょう。また、18) から 20) までは指示にしたがって解答しましょう。

1) hand out
 d_____
2) hand out
 g_____ out
3) in person
 f_____ to f_____
4) drop off
 d_____
5) drop off
 ⇔ p_____ up
6) prior to
 b_____
7) come up with
 c_____
8) come up with
 h_____ on
9) Feel free to 不定詞
 Don't h_____ to 不定詞
10) in time for
 not l_____ for

11) on display
 on s_____
12) be looking to 不定詞
 be p_____ to 不定詞
13) go over
 c_____
14) go over
 e_____
15) result in
 c_____
16) result in
 l_____ to
17) run out of
 u_____ up
18) note の形容詞形
 _____
19) depend の形容詞形
 _____
20) honor の形容詞形
 _____

# 今後頻出が予想される名詞・定型表現 46

| | | |
|---|---|---|
| 1. | landscaping<br>造園 | The **landscaping** company designed a rooftop garden for the office building.<br>その造園会社はそのオフィスビルに屋上庭園を設計した。 |
| 2. | account<br>顧客 | There is an opening for the position of **account** manager.<br>顧客担当部長の職位に空きがある。 |
| 3. | fund-raiser/fundraiser<br>資金集めのイベント | They're looking for volunteers for the city's charity **fund-raiser**.<br>彼らは市の慈善資金集めのイベントへのボランティアを募集している。 |
| 4. | post<br>投稿 | Matt regularly writes a blog **post** about his trips.<br>マットは定期的に旅行に関するブログの投稿をしている。 |
| 5. | textile<br>織物 | This is the factory and warehouse of the **textile** manufacturer.<br>ここはその織物メーカーの工場兼倉庫だ。 |
| 6. | initiative<br>新構想 | The company launched a strategic business **initiative** to recover its sales.<br>その会社は売上を回復するために戦略的な事業の新構想を開始した。 |
| 7. | craft<br>手工芸品 | There are several booths selling local **crafts** at the community fair.<br>その地域の見本市ではいくつかのブースが地元の手工芸品を販売している。 |
| 8. | item<br>項目 | The president added one more **item** to the meeting agenda.<br>社長は会議の議題に項目をもうひとつ加えた。 |
| 9. | prototype<br>試作品 | The developer demonstrated a **prototype** of the device at the board meeting.<br>その開発者は役員会議でそのデバイスの試作品を実演した。 |
| 10. | deal<br>お買い得品 | That supermarket chain advertises special **deals** every Tuesday.<br>そのスーパーマーケットチェーンは毎週火曜日に特別お買い得品を宣伝広告する。 |

今後頻出が予想される名詞・定型表現 46　127

| | | |
|---|---|---|
| 11. | **garment**<br>衣服 | These **garments** are made using a variety of fabrics.<br>これらの衣服はさまざまな布地で作られている。 |
| 12. | **hardware**<br>金物類 | The **hardware** store in the mall carries all kinds of tools.<br>ショッピングモールの金物店はあらゆる種類の道具を取り扱っている。 |
| 13. | **hospitality**<br>接客(業) | The restaurant's owner has a degree in **hospitality** management.<br>そのレストランのオーナーは接客業経営学の学位を持っている。 |
| 14. | **patron**<br>利用者 | The library notified **patrons** of the change in operating hours.<br>その図書館は利用者に開館時間の変更を通知した。 |
| 15. | **attachment**<br>添付(ファイル) | Fred sent his résumé as an email **attachment** to the firm.<br>フレッドは履歴書をメールに添付してその事務所に送った。 |
| 16. | **blueprint**<br>設計図 | The **blueprint** for the stadium was designed by the architecture firm.<br>その競技場の設計図はその建築事務所がデザインを担当した。 |
| 17. | **faculty**<br>教授陣 | The university's **faculty** are very good at their research.<br>その大学の教授陣は研究において非常にすぐれている。 |
| 18. | **networking**<br>人脈づくり | The seminar for smaller business owners provided a **networking** opportunity.<br>中小企業のオーナー対象のそのセミナーは人脈づくりの機会を提供した。 |
| 19. | **realty**<br>不動産 | Our **realty** company will value your property free of charge.<br>当不動産会社はお客さまの不動産を無料で査定いたします。 |
| 20. | **findings**<br>調査結果 | Anne presented the **findings** of the market analysis in the meeting.<br>アンは市場分析調査結果を会議でプレゼンした。 |

| | | |
|---|---|---|
| 21. | **furnishings**<br>家具 | The wallpaper in the living room matches the **furnishings**.<br>リビングのその壁紙は家具と合っている。 |
| 22. | **input**<br>意見 | Lucy's valuable **input** in the report helped us to select a new vendor.<br>報告書のルーシーの貴重な意見が、われわれが新しい供給業者を選ぶ助けとなった。 |
| 23. | **nursery**<br>園芸店 | The garden plants sold at the **nursery** are of excellent quality.<br>その園芸店で販売されている園芸用植物は質がすぐれている。 |
| 24. | **produce**<br>農産物 | Our grocery store offers fresh, local, organic **produce**.<br>当食料雑貨店は地元の新鮮な有機農産物を提供している。 |
| 25. | **reminder**<br>リマインダー<br>[再確認の連絡] | This is a friendly **reminder** of your appointment tomorrow at 3 pm.<br>これは明日午後3時のあなたの予約の念のためのリマインダーです。 |
| 26. | **bid**<br>入札(額) | We submitted a **bid** for the construction project.<br>われわれはその建設プロジェクトの入札額を提出した。 |
| 27. | **distributor**<br>卸売業者 | We shipped our new products to our contracted **distributors**.<br>当社が契約している卸売業者に新製品を出荷した。 |
| 28. | **profession**<br>職業 | Mike has been in the legal **profession** for years.<br>マイクは長年弁護士業に携わっている。 |
| 29. | **quote**<br>見積もり | Would you get **quotes** for the project from several advertising agencies?<br>複数の広告代理店からそのプロジェクトの見積もりを取ってもらえますか。 |
| 30. | **compensation**<br>報酬 | The general trading firm reviewed **compensation** for staff members.<br>その総合商社はスタッフの報酬を見直した。 |

今後頻出が予想される名詞・定型表現 46

| | | |
|---|---|---|
| 31. | **demolition**<br>取り壊し | The **demolition** of the city's famous old library has begun.<br>市の古い有名な図書館の取り壊しが始まった。 |
| 32. | **installment**<br>分割払い | Susie purchased her new vehicle on **installment**.<br>スージーは分割払いで新車を購入した。 |
| 33. | **outing**<br>小旅行 | Sally participated in the company **outing** last week.<br>サリーは先週会社の小旅行に参加した。 |
| 34. | **pottery**<br>陶磁器類 | The city museum has a unique collection of world **pottery**.<br>その市の美術館には他に類を見ない世界の陶磁器のコレクションがある。 |
| 35. | **facilitator**<br>司会者［進行役］ | The **facilitator** of the seminar had a lot of marketing expertise.<br>そのセミナーの司会者には市場戦略に関する多くの専門知識があった。 |
| 36. | **mentor**<br>新人指導者 | Bill was assigned as a **mentor** to the new employees.<br>ビルは新入社員の指導係に任命された。 |
| 37. | **moderator**<br>司会者［調整役］ | Ellen led the community forum as **moderator**.<br>エレンは司会者として地域の公開討論会を取り仕切った。 |
| 38. | **novice**<br>初級者 | David is a promising **novice** software developer.<br>デイビッドは将来有望なソフトウェア開発初級者だ。 |
| 39. | **quota**<br>ノルマ | George met his sales **quota** for three consecutive months.<br>ジョージは3か月連続で売上のノルマを達成した。 |
| 40. | **scheme**<br>配色 | Linda was very particular about the color **scheme** of her workroom.<br>リンダは自分の仕事部屋の配色にとてもこだわった。 |

| | | |
|---|---|---|
| 41. | focus group<br>フォーカスグループ [市場調査用に選ばれた消費者集団] | Feedback from the **focus group** was helpful in improving the product.<br>フォーカスグループからのフィードバックは商品の改良に役立った。 |
| 42. | overnight delivery/shipping<br>翌日配送 | We've just sent a replacement to you by **overnight delivery**.<br>代替品をお客さまに翌日配送でたった今お送りさせていただきました。 |
| 43. | professional development<br>職能開発 | We offer all employees many opportunities for **professional development**.<br>当社は全従業員に職能開発の多くの機会を提供している。 |
| 44. | keynote speaker<br>基調講演者 | Who would be the most appropriate **keynote speaker** for the convention?<br>大会の最もふさわしい基調講演者はどなたでしょうか。 |
| 45. | civil engineering<br>土木工学 | Ray specialized in **civil engineering** in graduate school.<br>レイは大学院で土木工学を専攻した。 |
| 46. | scheduling conflict<br>予定の重複 | Mary resolved some **scheduling conflicts** for the annual conference.<br>メアリはその年次大会の予定の重複をいくつか解決した。 |

# INDEX

* （見出し語句・表現）(Unit) －（Unit の1ページ目の番号）の順で表記
* ただし、63～64ページの語句は、（見出し語句）(P) －（番号）
  127～131ページの語句は、（見出し語句）(予) －（番号）の順で表記

- [ ] accept 6-19
- [ ] accommodate 21-17, 21-19
- [ ] accomplishment 22-20
- [ ] account 9-4, 13-3, 予-2
- [ ] accountant 20-3
- [ ] accounting 4-17
- [ ] accurately 29-19
- [ ] achievement 20-16
- [ ] actually 29-2
- [ ] add 2-14
- [ ] additional 8-3
- [ ] address 17-11
- [ ] adjust 12-20
- [ ] administrative 23-18
- [ ] administrator 26-14
- [ ] admission 18-5
- [ ] advanced 19-5
- [ ] advertise 6-1
- [ ] advertisement 3-1
- [ ] advertising 1-15
- [ ] affordable 19-15
- [ ] agency 4-18
- [ ] agenda 13-12
- [ ] agent 13-13
- [ ] agreement 11-17
- [ ] aisle 18-14
- [ ] alternate 27-11
- [ ] amount 5-12
- [ ] analysis 22-12
- [ ] anniversary 11-10
- [ ] annual 8-7
- [ ] anticipate 17-20
- [ ] apologize (for) 17-7
- [ ] app 5-13
- [ ] appliance 11-2
- [ ] applicant 16-7

- [ ] application 4-20
- [ ] apply (for) 6-17
- [ ] apply (to) 21-1
- [ ] appointment 1-18
- [ ] appreciate 21-7
- [ ] appreciation 24-1
- [ ] appropriate 27-17
- [ ] approval 22-13
- [ ] approve 6-11
- [ ] approximately 29-11
- [ ] architect 16-8
- [ ] architecture 28-10
- [ ] arrange 10-1, P-11
- [ ] arrangement 16-9
- [ ] article 1-19
- [ ] as of 30-13
- [ ] assemble P-12
- [ ] assembly line 14-12
- [ ] assign 12-8
- [ ] assignment 7-14
- [ ] assistance 11-3
- [ ] associate 16-17
- [ ] association 20-17
- [ ] attach 17-16
- [ ] attachment 予-15
- [ ] attend 2-5
- [ ] attendee 13-4
- [ ] attract 10-5
- [ ] attractive 23-6
- [ ] auditorium 28-11
- [ ] author 7-7
- [ ] automobile 7-3
- [ ] available 8-1, 8-12
- [ ] award 3-2
- [ ] baggage claim 14-14
- [ ] banquet 9-9
- [ ] be familiar with 15-17

- [ ] be honored to 不定詞 30-17
- [ ] be in charge of 15-19
- [ ] be intended for 15-11
- [ ] be likely to 不定詞 30-3
- [ ] be located (in/on/etc) 15-2
- [ ] be looking to 不定詞 30-14
- [ ] be subject to 名詞 30-20
- [ ] be supposed to 不定詞 15-12
- [ ] be willing to 不定詞 15-15
- [ ] benefits 13-17
- [ ] beverage 11-4
- [ ] bid 予-26
- [ ] bill 7-20
- [ ] blueprint 予-16
- [ ] board 13-5
- [ ] board of directors 14-6
- [ ] book 10-7
- [ ] botanical garden 14-10
- [ ] box office 14-15
- [ ] branch 9-17
- [ ] broadcast 20-9
- [ ] brochure 9-1
- [ ] budget 1-11
- [ ] bulletin board 14-16
- [ ] candidate 5-1
- [ ] career 7-8
- [ ] carry 21-20
- [ ] cashier P-4
- [ ] caterer 24-2
- [ ] catering 9-10
- [ ] ceiling P-2
- [ ] celebration 7-4
- [ ] certificate 20-18
- [ ] challenging 23-19
- [ ] charge 9-11, 12-9
- [ ] city hall 14-11

INDEX 133

- [ ] civil engineering 予-45
- [ ] client 1-4
- [ ] clothing 4-5
- [ ] colleague 3-15
- [ ] come up with 30-7
- [ ] commercial 19-16
- [ ] commitment 24-19
- [ ] committee 18-15
- [ ] community 3-16
- [ ] compensation 予-30
- [ ] competition 13-18, 24-20
- [ ] competitive 23-7
- [ ] competitor 13-6
- [ ] complaint 13-7
- [ ] complete 2-7
- [ ] complex 20-4
- [ ] complimentary 8-19
- [ ] concerned 8-10
- [ ] conduct 2-12
- [ ] conference 1-5
- [ ] conference call 14-8
- [ ] confident 23-20
- [ ] confirm 2-18
- [ ] confirmation 11-5
- [ ] consequently 29-20
- [ ] consistently 29-17
- [ ] construction 3-8
- [ ] consumer 18-16
- [ ] contact information 14-3
- [ ] contain 10-17
- [ ] container 20-10
- [ ] contract 1-16
- [ ] contractor 24-3
- [ ] convention 5-18
- [ ] corporate 8-11
- [ ] correct 12-2
- [ ] council 11-11
- [ ] coworker 11-12
- [ ] craft 予-7
- [ ] crew 13-19
- [ ] critic 24-8
- [ ] critical 27-18
- [ ] culinary 27-1
- [ ] currently 29-1

- [ ] customer 1-3
- [ ] deadline 3-18
- [ ] deal 26-15, 予-10
- [ ] decade 24-4
- [ ] defect 26-1
- [ ] defective 27-19
- [ ] definitely 29-7
- [ ] degree 20-19
- [ ] delay 7-15, 10-13
- [ ] deliver 6-6
- [ ] demand 20-20
- [ ] demolition 予-31
- [ ] demonstrate 25-1
- [ ] dental 23-8
- [ ] department 1-7
- [ ] departure 24-9
- [ ] depend on 30-12
- [ ] deposit 22-1
- [ ] description 13-14
- [ ] destination 24-10
- [ ] detail 4-11
- [ ] develop 10-16
- [ ] developer 18-6
- [ ] development 5-19
- [ ] device 5-14
- [ ] directions 20-5
- [ ] directory 26-16
- [ ] distribute 12-15
- [ ] distributor 予-27
- [ ] district 24-11
- [ ] division 22-14
- [ ] document 3-12
- [ ] donate 17-8
- [ ] donation 11-18
- [ ] doorway P-5
- [ ] draft 22-15
- [ ] drawer P-1
- [ ] drop off 30-4
- [ ] due 8-15
- [ ] due to 名詞 15-14
- [ ] durable 23-9
- [ ] duty 24-5
- [ ] eager 23-12
- [ ] edit 17-3

- [ ] editor 9-5
- [ ] electricity 22-16
- [ ] electronic 8-16
- [ ] electronics 11-13
- [ ] eligible 27-2
- [ ] emphasize 25-2
- [ ] employee 1-1
- [ ] employer 28-12
- [ ] employment 18-7
- [ ] employment agency 14-7
- [ ] enclose 25-15
- [ ] encourage 6-4
- [ ] enroll (in) 21-2
- [ ] enrollment 28-13
- [ ] ensure 12-3
- [ ] enthusiastic 27-12
- [ ] envelope 28-14
- [ ] equipment 1-8
- [ ] establish 21-8
- [ ] estimate 5-15, 21-9
- [ ] evaluate 25-3
- [ ] eventually 29-13
- [ ] exactly 29-12
- [ ] exceed 25-4
- [ ] exclusive 27-13
- [ ] executive 24-12
- [ ] exhibit 18-17
- [ ] exhibition 11-19
- [ ] expand 10-6
- [ ] expect 2-20, 21-3
- [ ] expense 5-8
- [ ] experienced 19-3
- [ ] expert 11-20
- [ ] expertise 26-2
- [ ] expire 25-5
- [ ] expo 13-8
- [ ] express 19-6
- [ ] extend 10-3
- [ ] extended 23-13
- [ ] extension 28-15
- [ ] extensive 19-20
- [ ] extra 8-6
- [ ] extremely 29-10
- [ ] fabric 18-8

- [ ] facilitator 予-35
- [ ] facility 3-9
- [ ] faculty 予-17
- [ ] fair 7-17
- [ ] fare 26-3
- [ ] feature 5-9, 6-15
- [ ] fee 3-3
- [ ] feedback 4-10
- [ ] feel free to 不定詞 30-8
- [ ] fill out 15-7
- [ ] finance 11-6
- [ ] financial 8-5
- [ ] findings 予-20
- [ ] firm 3-13
- [ ] fix 10-18
- [ ] flexible 27-3
- [ ] flyer 18-18
- [ ] focus group 予-41
- [ ] fold P-14
- [ ] following 8-13
- [ ] form 1-10
- [ ] former 27-4
- [ ] forward 25-19
- [ ] founder 24-6
- [ ] fund 16-10
- [ ] fund-raiser/fundraiser 予-3
- [ ] fund-raising/fundraising 23-1
- [ ] furnishings 予-21
- [ ] gallery 7-11
- [ ] garment 予-11
- [ ] generous 27-5
- [ ] gift certificate 14-18
- [ ] given 名詞/that 節 15-20
- [ ] go over 30-15
- [ ] grocery store 14-5
- [ ] guarantee 17-12
- [ ] guidelines 28-16
- [ ] hand out 30-1
- [ ] handle 17-17
- [ ] hang P-9
- [ ] hardware 予-12
- [ ] headquarters 13-9
- [ ] highlight 21-18
- [ ] highly 29-5
- [ ] hire 2-4
- [ ] hospitality 予-13
- [ ] host 6-7
- [ ] human resources 14-1
- [ ] ideal 23-2
- [ ] identification 4-14
- [ ] image 11-7
- [ ] implement 21-15
- [ ] imply 17-4
- [ ] impressed 23-10
- [ ] improve 6-8
- [ ] improvement 13-15
- [ ] in advance 15-8
- [ ] in person 30-2
- [ ] in stock 15-13
- [ ] in time (for) 30-9
- [ ] include 2-3
- [ ] increase 6-2
- [ ] indicate 2-17
- [ ] individual 27-6, 28-1
- [ ] industrial 19-17
- [ ] industry 4-15
- [ ] inexpensive 19-4
- [ ] inform 6-18
- [ ] ingredient 13-20
- [ ] initial 23-14
- [ ] initiative 予-6
- [ ] innovative 19-10
- [ ] input 予-22
- [ ] inquire (about) 12-16
- [ ] inquiry 24-13
- [ ] inspect 17-9
- [ ] inspection 7-12
- [ ] inspector 18-9
- [ ] install 6-13
- [ ] installment 予-32
- [ ] instructions 9-2, 16-11
- [ ] instrument 22-2
- [ ] insurance 22-3
- [ ] intern 20-11
- [ ] interview 4-6
- [ ] inventory 9-3
- [ ] invest (in) 21-10
- [ ] investment 20-6
- [ ] invitaion 7-16
- [ ] invoice 5-4
- [ ] involve 21-11
- [ ] issue 16-12, 16-18, 21-16
- [ ] item 1-6, 予-8
- [ ] itinerary 16-19
- [ ] keynote speaker 予-44
- [ ] laboratory 11-8
- [ ] ladder P-6
- [ ] landmark 26-17
- [ ] landscaping 予-1
- [ ] laptop 7-9
- [ ] latest 8-17
- [ ] launch 21-12, 22-17
- [ ] lead 6-3
- [ ] leading 27-7
- [ ] lean against P-17
- [ ] legal 19-18
- [ ] line 7-13
- [ ] load 17-18
- [ ] local 8-2
- [ ] location 1-9, 3-19
- [ ] luggage 11-9
- [ ] maintain 17-19
- [ ] maintenance 4-1
- [ ] make sure that 節／be sure to 不定詞 15-4
- [ ] manage 12-13
- [ ] management 5-10, 13-16
- [ ] manufacture 21-13
- [ ] manufacturer 7-10
- [ ] marketing 1-14
- [ ] material 3-4, 5-20
- [ ] mayor 16-20
- [ ] medical 8-9
- [ ] medication 24-14
- [ ] meet 10-14
- [ ] memo 13-1
- [ ] mention 6-9
- [ ] mentor 予-36
- [ ] merchandise 5-5
- [ ] merger 11-14
- [ ] minutes 28-17

- miss 12-18
- missing 8-20
- mobile 19-7
- moderator 予-37
- monitor 25-6
- multiple 19-1
- nearly 29-8
- negotiate 25-10
- networking 予-18
- newsletter 18-1
- notice 4-7
- notify 17-1
- novice 予-38
- nursery 予-23
- nutrition 28-18
- obtain 12-17
- offer 2-1
- official 20-7
- on behalf of 30-18
- on display 30-10
- on time 15-9
- online 8-4
- on-site 19-8
- opening 16-1
- operate 25-7, 25-11
- operation 16-2
- opportunity 4-8
- option 4-9
- order 2-13
- organization 16-3
- organize 10-10
- organizer 26-4
- outing 予-33
- outstanding 19-11
- overnight delivery/shipping 予-42
- overtime 28-19
- own 12-4
- package 4-12, 7-1
- packaging 5-11
- paperwork 13-2
- participant 4-19
- participate (in) 6-16
- passenger 7-18

- patient 9-18
- patron 予-14
- payment 3-6
- payroll 18-2
- performance 9-12, 20-12
- permission 18-10
- permit 18-11
- personnel 24-7
- pharmacy 16-4
- pick up 15-1
- pile P-13
- place an order (for) 15-10
- Please note that 節 30-5
- policy 1-13
- position 1-12
- positive 23-15
- post 10-12, 予-4
- postal 27-8
- postpone 17-2
- potential 8-14
- pottery 予-34
- pour P-15
- power 16-13
- predict 25-8
- preference 26-5
- prescription 26-6
- present 12-10
- press conference 14-9
- press release 14-19
- previously 29-3
- prior to 名詞 30-6
- priority 26-18
- procedure 9-19
- process 12-6
- produce 12-11, 予-24
- product 1-2
- production 3-17
- profession 予-28
- professional development 予-43
- professor 18-3
- progress 26-7
- promote 6-20, 25-16
- promotion 9-13, 22-4

- properly 29-6
- property 4-13
- proposal 5-2
- propose 12-5
- prospective 23-11
- prototype 予-9
- provide 2-2
- public relations 14-17
- publication 18-19
- publicity 28-2
- publish 10-19
- purchase 2-6, 3-10
- put away P-18
- qualification 28-3
- qualified 19-12
- quality 23-3
- quality control 14-20
- quantity 20-13
- quarter 7-2
- questionnaire 26-8
- quota 予-39
- quote 予-29
- raise 25-12
- rate 13-10
- real eatate 14-2
- realty 予-19
- reasonable 27-14
- receipt 7-19
- reception 18-20
- receptionist 26-19
- recipe 7-5
- recipient 28-4
- recognize 25-13
- recommend 2-16
- recommendation 18-12
- recruit 12-19
- reduce 2-19
- reduced 23-16
- reference 16-5
- reflect 25-17
- refreshments 20-1
- refrigerator 20-14
- refund 5-16
- region 16-14

- [ ] regional 19-19
- [ ] register (for) 10-4
- [ ] registration 9-14
- [ ] regularly 29-9
- [ ] regulation 20-15
- [ ] reimbursement 28-5
- [ ] related 19-14
- [ ] relatively 29-18
- [ ] relevant 27-15
- [ ] relocate 17-6
- [ ] remind 10-8
- [ ] reminder 予-25
- [ ] remove 10-2
- [ ] renew 17-10
- [ ] renovate 10-20
- [ ] renovation 5-3
- [ ] rent 10-11
- [ ] repair 6-14
- [ ] replace 6-12
- [ ] replacement 11-15
- [ ] representative 5-6
- [ ] require 2-10
- [ ] requirement 16-15
- [ ] reschedule 12-1
- [ ] reservation 1-20
- [ ] reserve 6-10
- [ ] resident 5-7
- [ ] resistant 27-20
- [ ] resources 22-5
- [ ] respond (to) 12-7
- [ ] response 13-11
- [ ] restore 25-18
- [ ] result in 30-16
- [ ] résumé 9-15
- [ ] retail 8-18
- [ ] retailer 26-9
- [ ] revenue 22-6
- [ ] review 2-15, 3-7, 25-14, 26-10
- [ ] revise 6-5
- [ ] reward 26-20
- [ ] role 22-7
- [ ] run 21-4
- [ ] run out of 30-19

- [ ] sales figures 14-13
- [ ] scheduling conflict 予-46
- [ ] scheme 予-40
- [ ] sculpture 26-11
- [ ] secure 23-17
- [ ] security 4-2
- [ ] seek 17-13
- [ ] selection 22-18
- [ ] senior 23-4
- [ ] serve 17-5
- [ ] server 22-8
- [ ] session 4-3
- [ ] set up 15-3
- [ ] ship 12-12
- [ ] shipment 4-16
- [ ] shipping 3-14
- [ ] shortly 29-14
- [ ] sign P-7
- [ ] sign up (for) 15-5
- [ ] significant 27-9
- [ ] solution 20-2
- [ ] source 22-9
- [ ] specialize (in) 12-14
- [ ] specifications 28-6
- [ ] spokesperson 24-15
- [ ] stack P-10
- [ ] stairs P-3
- [ ] statement 24-16, 26-12
- [ ] status 22-10
- [ ] steps P-8
- [ ] stop by 15-16
- [ ] storage 9-6
- [ ] store 17-14
- [ ] strategy 16-6
- [ ] submit 2-9
- [ ] subscriber 20-8
- [ ] subscription 18-13
- [ ] suggest 2-11, 10-9
- [ ] suggestion 9-20
- [ ] suitable 23-5
- [ ] summary 22-11
- [ ] supervise 25-9
- [ ] supervisor 4-4
- [ ] supplier 18-4

- [ ] supplies 3-11
- [ ] survey 1-17
- [ ] sustainable 27-16
- [ ] sweep P-16
- [ ] take over 30-11
- [ ] task 9-16
- [ ] technical 19-2
- [ ] temporary 19-9
- [ ] tenant 24-17
- [ ] tentatively 29-15
- [ ] terms 26-13
- [ ] textile 予-5
- [ ] thoroughly 29-16
- [ ] tip 22-19
- [ ] track 21-5
- [ ] trade show 14-4
- [ ] traffic 9-7
- [ ] trail 7-6
- [ ] transaction 28-7
- [ ] transfer 25-20
- [ ] transition 28-8
- [ ] transportation 5-17
- [ ] under construction P-19
- [ ] undergo 21-14
- [ ] unfortunately 29-4
- [ ] up to 名詞 15-18
- [ ] upcoming 8-8
- [ ] update 2-8, 11-16
- [ ] urgent 27-10
- [ ] valid 19-13
- [ ] vehicle 3-20
- [ ] vending machine P-20
- [ ] vendor 16-16
- [ ] venue 24-18
- [ ] verify 21-6
- [ ] vote 17-15
- [ ] voucher 28-9
- [ ] warehouse 9-8
- [ ] warranty 11-1
- [ ] wildlife 28-20
- [ ] win 10-15
- [ ] work on 15-6
- [ ] workshop 3-5

Copyright © 2025 by
Osamu Inoue, Paul Leeming, Narumi Yoshino, Justin Harris
and TSURUMI SHOTEN

All rights reserved

---

**完全改訂版**

### TOEIC® Test 単語　頻度順徹底マスター
スコア450➡550➡650をめざす600+66の語と表現

| 編著者 | 井上　治 |
| --- | --- |
| | Paul Leeming |
| | 吉野　成美 |
| | Justin Harris |
| 発行者 | 山口　隆史 |
| 発行所 | 株式会社 音羽書房鶴見書店 |

〒113-0033　東京都文京区本郷 3-26-13
TEL 03-3814-0491
FAX 03-3814-9250
URL: https://www.otowatsurumi.com
e-mail: info@otowatsurumi.com

2025年3月1日　初版発行

---

組版　ほんのしろ
装幀　吉成美佐（オセロ）
印刷・製本　（株）シナノ パブリッシング プレス
■ 落丁・乱丁本はお取り替えいたします。　　EC-078